You'd
Some Ice On That

Juanita Broaddrick

with Nick Lulli

ISBN: 1979834245
ISBN-13: 978-1979834247

Photos, videos, and documents are available at JuanitaBroaddrick.com

DEDICATION

For my son, Kevin. You have always stood beside me and supported me. You taught me more about truth and honor than I was ever able to teach you.

CONTENTS

FOREWORD

We'll just come out and say it: in 1978, Bill Clinton raped Juanita Broaddrick. See the period there? End of story. Yes, it was rape. It's a traumatic event that for the scores of women and men who face it every year, is never forgotten.

To the political world, a sexual assault can act as a partisan tool to wield against one's opponent. To the victims, it's real. Bill Clinton's egregious past abuse of women has burst back into the public consciousness due to some equally egregious actions by other powerful men. Suddenly, the New York Times is blaring, "I Believe Juanita."[1] Even Democratic Senator Kirsten Gillibrand has declared Bill Clinton should have resigned over the Lewinsky scandal.[2] Did she forget Juanita Broaddrick, Paula Jones, and Kathleen Willey? If consensual sex with a 22-year-old intern and perjury equals resignation, what does sexual assault equal? Prison?

This sudden shift in values is too little, too late. Now that the Clintons are in their waning days, suddenly it's open season. Where was this thinking when the Clinton machine was viciously attacking the victims? "Bimbo eruptions."[3] How crude.

Even more appalling, Hillary Rodham Clinton's continued false statements (read: lies) about her husband's sex abuse.

In November 2017 on WABC Radio, while attacking Roy Moore and Donald Trump, she declared about Bill's incidents, "Look, I think every

---

[1] Goldberg, M. (2017, November 13). I Believe Juanita. Retrieved November 19, 2017, from https://www.nytimes.com/2017/11/13/opinion/juanita-broaddrick-bill-clinton.html

[2] Rosenberg, E. (2017, November 17). Kirsten Gillibrand says Bill Clinton should have resigned, as old allegations resurface. Retrieved November 19, 2017, from https://www.washingtonpost.com/news/politics/wp/2017/11/17/kirsten-gillibrand-says-bill-clinton-should-have-resigned-as-old-allegations-resurface/

[3] Boburg, S. (2016, September 28). Enabler or family defender? How Hillary Clinton responded to husband's accusers. Retrieved November 19, 2017, from https://www.washingtonpost.com/local/enabler-or-family-defender-how-hillary-clinton-responded-to-husbands-accusers/2016/09/28/58dad5d4-6fb1-11e6-8533-6b0b0ded0253_story.html?utm_term=.50c305d25b0b

situation has to be judged on its own merit, and there were allegations that were disproved."[4]

On the contrary, the allegations were not disproved. Her husband willingly paid a six-figure settlement to Paula Jones after he exposed himself to her.[5] The Broaddrick case was cast off with a curt statement in 1999 by the Clintons' lawyer.[6]

That's why we are publishing this book. The record will be set straight once and for all. And if you're wondering about the title? That's what Bill Clinton said to shaken and shell-shocked Juanita after his horrific attack on her was over. In her own words, Juanita will be telling her story in full without the filter of the media. She will be able to recount her horrific experience without her words being chopped on the cutting room floor. We're not the Clintons here; there's no lucrative book advance (it's being self-published). This is an effort meant to make sure the next generation knows what happened.

The 1999 Dateline interview discussing the Broaddrick rape was intentionally held by NBC until after Bill Clinton's impeachment trial. With the current climate, we're optimistic the media will be a little more open. The more people who are allowed to speak about their assaults, the quicker more victims will open up and begin the healing process so desperately needed.

But even now we're seeing some inaccuracies, either willful or unintentional. Some media outlets are airing reports that the president was adjudicated one way or another for his actions.[7] There continues to be a salacious obsession with Monica Lewinsky. While that in itself is a form of

---

[4] Posted By Ian Schwartz On Date November 18, 2017. (n.d.). Clinton: We Have A Man Accused Of Sexual Assault Sitting In The Oval Office, Accusations Not Taken Seriously. Retrieved November 19, 2017, from
https://www.realclearpolitics.com/video/2017/11/18/hillary_clinton_we_have_a_man_accused_of_sex ual_assault_sitting_in_the_oval_office_accusations_not_taken_seriously.html

[5] DAVID G. SAVAGE | TIMES STAFF WRITER. (1998, November 14). Clinton Will Pay $850,000 to End Paula Jones Suit. Retrieved November 19, 2017, from
http://articles.latimes.com/1998/nov/14/news/mn-42627

[6] Matthews, D. (2016, January 06). The rape allegation against Bill Clinton, explained. Retrieved November 19, 2017, from https://www.vox.com/2016/1/6/10722580/bill-clinton-juanita-broaddrick

[7] Diaz, D. (2017, November 18). Panetta on Lewinsky affair: Bill Clinton 'more than paid the price'. Retrieved November 19, 2017, from http://www.cnn.com/2017/11/18/politics/leon-panetta-hillary-clinton-kirsten-gillibrand/index.html

sexual abuse (a much older 'boss' figure taking advantage of a willing participant), it pales in comparison to what other women have gone through. Why are we not leading every Clinton story with the former president raping Juanita? Why are we not leading them with the former president exposing his penis to Paula Jones, asking her to "kiss it?" And, why are we not leading the stories with Kathleen Willey being groped in the White House?

As Mrs. Clinton herself once urged, "Every survivor of sexual assault deserves to be heard, believed, and supported."[8]

We agree.

.

---

[8] Clinton, H. (2015, November 23). Every survivor of sexual assault deserves to be heard, believed, and supported. https://t.co/mkD69RHeBL. Retrieved November 19, 2017, from https://twitter.com/hillaryclinton/status/668597149291184128?lang=en

IT WAS RAPE

What in God's name had just happened? I was brutally raped, my lip was throbbing and hurting as well as other parts of my body, and I was frightened to death. I had this overwhelming feeling that someone might come in to get rid of the "body." That's what I felt like......a body. I went to the door and locked it and went back to the bed and laid down. I didn't want to move or look in the mirror at the injuries. I must have laid there an hour or more before I heard a knock at the door. When I looked through the peephole, I saw Norma. Dear God, I had completely forgotten about her and the seminar. I had just wanted to go to sleep and wake up from this bad dream. When I opened the door and saw the look on her face, I started crying all over again.

I speak from personal experience when I say victims of sexual and/or physical abuse do not want to shout out the lurid details of their abuse from the mountain top. They want to curl up in a fetal position and pray it won't happen again. Sadly, it does. Like the hundreds of men and women who messaged me on Twitter and Facebook during the 2016 Presidential campaign to tell me their own stories of abuse, I was ashamed and thought it was my fault. On the contrary, it was not our fault. I hope my story will help other victims come forward and report the abuse to authorities, or at best, talk to someone they trust. I understand the reluctance. This book is the first time I have written in detail about my abuses that happened decades ago.

My assaults were by two people whom you do not normally think of as abusive: my mother and a public figure who became the President of the United States.

MY EARLY YEARS

I have always believed my mother was ashamed of the mental and physical abuse she committed on my sister, my dad and I, but being ashamed wasn't enough to stop it. There was never any rhyme or reasoning to her abuse. My sister, Patsy, and I were the subjects of her physical abuse and my dad suffered from her verbal and emotional abuse. The tantrums would suddenly erupt and then disappear as quickly as they came. My father was a good man, but he never protected my sister and I like I thought a father should. I wanted him to do something, just anything, to intervene and stop the abuse. Still, we adored our dad because he was so kind and always there to console us after these outbursts. She seemed to view his actions as a betrayal and would say "There's something I will tell you about your dad that will make you hate him." We heard this statement over and over again. Then one night she blurted it out.

It was the night of Thursday, December 22, 1955. I was 13 and Patsy was 15. Dad left home to play cards with his weekly men's group at the country club. I say country club loosely. There was a nine hole golf course and a small building for golfers to store their gear and a kitchen dining area. If you wanted food and/or drinks, you had to bring your own. My sister and I had plans with friends and left shortly after dad. I was the first to return home about 8:30 p.m. The first thing to catch my eye was our beautiful Christmas tree but it wasn't shining brightly through the front window. Instead, it was lying in the front yard, along with all of the beautifully wrapped presents and decorations strewn in every direction. My first thought was "I'm not about to go in there alone." I sat on the porch and waited for dad and sis to come home.

I remember it was cold as I sat there, waiting for the reinforcements to arrive. Patsy got there first and then dad. We just looked at each other, not knowing whether to start picking up everything or to venture inside. We settled for the latter. It was serious back then, but now, for some crazy reason, it amuses me, like a scene from the movie, A Christmas Story. It was three days before Christmas and our beautiful tree and all our presents were sprawled on the ground in the front yard….. and it was raining!

She was sitting in the living room, waiting for us. It had been a few weeks since her last episode. She just sat there on the couch with that look we knew so well. Her face was flushed and wet with tears. Tears always accompanied her anger. Then she said, "Your dad never married me until I was pregnant with Juanita and Patsy was 2." Okay, now what does a young teenager do with that statement? Today, a lot of marriages take place after children are born and sometimes not at all, but in 1942 when I was born, it was a rare occurrence. Patsy turned to dad and said, "Are you my dad?" He answered, "Absolutely." I don't think she believed him and she ran out the front door to her friend's home a block away. That long dreaded revelation affected me differently. It was finally out in the open. I thought, "What's the big deal?" It was certainly not as bad as she had built it up to be in my mind all these years. Still, I was not the one who was slapped in the face with paternal doubts.

Usually these episodes would happen in privacy inside our home but not outside for everyone to see. As far as I knew, the neighbors were unaware of what went on inside the home at 1616 Cherry Street, Van Buren, Arkansas. Mom would inflict havoc on us and then retreat to her bedroom. That's what happened on this evening, leaving dad and I to "tidy up" before the neighbors saw it. It was a total mess. Our front porch was too small to put the remnants of this epic disaster so Dad moved the car out of the garage so we could put everything in there and out of sight. I remember him muttering he shouldn't have left her alone, because he knew she was upset about something. I thought to myself, "What the Hell," but, of course, I didn't say it. Even back, then at my young age, I knew, he knew, it wasn't his fault. He always wanted everything to be okay, but things weren't okay, no matter how much blame he felt obligated to accept. He tried to hide it, but I could see the tears he continually wiped away. I hurt for him and wanted to console him, but I didn't know how. I had never seen dad cry anything but happy tears. When he laughed, the tears would flow. I inherited that from him.

When I was born, my mother, at the age of 22, had a total hysterectomy, removing her fallopian tubes, ovaries and uterus. She was not given any hormonal replacement therapy. Just stripped and sent home. Being a nurse, I have always wondered if this could have triggered her terrible mood swings or if perhaps she might have been bipolar. There had to be a reason for her behavior. She also suffered from severe migraine headaches and every few weeks she would be completely incapacitated for 2-3 days at a time. She seemed to be in excruciating pain lying in a darkened bedroom. I felt sorry for her. Our family physician, Dr. Savery, lived next door and he would come to our house and give her injections for the pain. I also suffered from migraine headaches and like her, the headaches went away in my fifties.

So now let's go back to my earlier years. When I was very young, from the age of about 2 to 8, I was very frightened of my mom. I wet the bed until I was five years old, but this never seemed to upset her. She would calmly change my pajamas and the linens and tell me it would get better someday. I was so ashamed. But then, at other times and for absolutely no reason, she would slap me in the face or pull my hair or both, with no explanation of what I had done to provoke her. One evening after dinner, when I was about 5 or 6, my mom grabbed me by my hair. I got free from her and grabbed a large butcher knife from the drawer. I guess I wanted to defend myself. My dad immediately swooped me up and carried me to the backyard. I can actually remember saying that I was going to kill her. What a terrible memory for a child to have. My dad took the knife from me and rocked me for a long time in one of our lawn rockers. I do not remember anything else about that

14

night.

When I was approximately 9 or 10 years old, I came home from school one day to find my mother had taken a crowbar and ripped all the kitchen cabinets off the wall and the kitchen was a disaster. She was only about 5 feet tall and weighed about 100 pounds but when she set her mind to do something, you would have thought she was 200 pounds and 6 feet tall. The previous night, I overheard her talking to dad about remodeling the kitchen. I vaguely remember him saying they couldn't afford it right now or something to that effect. That afternoon was a turning point in my young life.

As soon as I walked into the kitchen, she must have seen the startled look on my face and didn't like it. She came toward me and I knew "it" was going to happen. I had already surpassed her in weight and height being big for my age. She tried to hit me and I dodged. Then to my surprise, I grabbed her and threw her to the floor. I screamed at her "Don't you every hit me again." It shocked me as much as it did her, but I felt victorious. Fighting back had never been in my realm of thought. It just happened. Looking back, I am not proud of my actions. I remember in Sunday school they would say honor thy father and thy mother but where was honor thy children? From that day forward she never hit me again, but, of course, she would disparage me. My sister became her target for slaps and hair pulling for the next couple of years. Then, suddenly, the physical abuse stopped. I was so relieved for my sister but disappointed she never resisted during those two years. She was a head taller and 50 pounds heavier than mother. She was big for her age, too.

There were good times. It's sad that all the bad memories overshadow them. We would take weeklong vacations every summer in the early 1950's. For some reason, mom never had any episodes during these wonderful trips. We would drive along the old Route 66 to California and then the following years to New York, Canada and Florida. Route 66 and all the iconic displays along the way was my favorite, except for Carlsbad Caverns. I was afraid and couldn't go in the caverns with them. I had a fear of the dark and closed spaces and always had to have the light on when I went to bed at night.

These fears and phobias would grow worse in my thirties. There were only four summer vacations but I remember them as though it was yesterday. Several years ago, I found an old postcard dad had sent to his employees at his business. It was a photo of the Grand Canyon and scrawled on the back were descriptions of all the sights and sheer joy we were experiencing. Holding and reading his words, I floated back in my mind to 1954 and I smiled. I am so glad I have those memories of the good times we shared together.

As I said in the beginning I think my mother was ashamed of her actions. Usually a day or two following each slap or hair pulling episode, she would take my sister and I shopping. In her own way I think she was saying, "I'm sorry." She rarely bought anything for herself but always made sure my sis and I had nice clothes to wear. She got up very early most mornings to cook a huge meal for dinner and put it in the oven to keep warm. Then, she would do the laundry and hang it outside on the clothesline. I have no idea how the food kept from petrifying, but it was always delicious when we removed it from the oven for dinner. She was a fabulous cook. Patsy and I would get the laundry from the clothesline after school. In the winter, the clothes would be stiff and frozen and we had to lay them on the back sunporch until they thawed. Mom did all the housework. She was always busy. We were spoiled when it came to chores around the house. I always thought this was just another way to make up for her behavior. We would have gladly traded doing housework and new clothes in lieu of the abuse.

After we left for school, mom would join my dad at their Dry Cleaning business and work with him until 6 p.m. most days. The cleaners was four blocks from my school and home was five blocks from the cleaners. When I was in grade school, I walked by the cleaners on my way home, so I would usually stop and go thru the "junk box." The junk box was a medium size cardboard box full of items left in peoples clothing. A smaller box of recent items was left on the counter for customers to look through for lost articles. If no one claimed these items after a month, the contents would be emptied into the large junk box kept in the corner by the sewing machine. When I say junk, I mean junk, but it was exciting for a kid to go through. It contained buttons, pocketknives, hair berets, very small plastic and rubber toys, coins and so much more. Mom would be busy waiting on customers or pressing clothes. I would sit on the floor in the corner by the sewing machine, searching for my special treasure. Mostly, I loved watching her. She would smile and laugh with the customers and employees. She was so happy there. This was the mother any child would adore. Sometimes she would look at me with one of those smiles. On the walk home, I would wonder if she really meant to smile at me or if it was just residual from talking to a customer.

The cleaners was open 7 a.m. to 6 p.m. Monday through Friday and Saturday till 7 p.m. If it was a school holiday or Saturday, the local movie theaters were our babysitters, starting when I was about 6 years old. Patsy and I would catch the bus on the corner by our home and go to the Bob Burns Theater in Van Buren, or across the Arkansas River to Fort Smith to the Joie or the Malco Theater. One Saturday a month, admission was one can goods in lieu of the $.20 admission. Mom would put two cans of food in a brown paper bag for Patsy to carry. Sometimes, Patsy would get money out of her piggy bank and put the cans back in the pantry, so she wouldn't have to carry them.

I loved the old Joie because it was decorated lavishly and had a beautiful stairway that went upstairs to a large open lobby with lounge furniture and restrooms. It had over 1200 seats and a beautiful stage. The Bob Burns (named after the humorist and film star of the 1940s) and the Malco were much smaller. My sister and I would stay at the theater all afternoon, watching the same movie over and over before catching the last bus back home. We knew so much about the movie stars of the 1940s-50s and could immediately name any one of them if given the name of the movie.

According to my high school yearbooks, I was very involved in school activities. I was a cheerleader from junior high all the way through senior high. I was elected to student council and became student body president my senior year. I was voted best all around, runner up to most beautiful and most talented and FFA Sweetheart. I loved to sing and entered a lot of beauty pageants that required talent competition. I was Miss Van Buren, a contestant in the Miss Arkansas pageant and Miss Congeniality at the Arkansas Jr. Miss pageant. Now, as I reflect back on these years, I remember all my feelings of insecurity and self-doubt. Instead of enjoying what seemed to be a high school girl's dream, I just muddled through my young life. A few years ago, my class of 1960 had a 50 year reunion. I was simply amazed by what my former classmates told me. They said things like, "How smart I was and what a great leader I was." Surely they had me confused with someone else. That is not the girl I remember.

WHO WANTS TO BE A NURSE?

I never wanted to be a nurse. I wanted a career in entertainment. I auditioned for and received a vocal scholarship at the College of the Ozarks, but my father would not allow me to go in this direction saying it was frivolous. There were two nursing schools in my area, Sparks Memorial and St. Edwards, and each offered the old 3 year diploma program. It was August of 1960 and not wanting to lose a year of education, I applied for Sparks School of Nursing and was accepted. My sister had just graduated from St Edwards School of nursing and I remember hearing her complaints about the nuns in charge of her school, so I chose Sparks. I hadn't planned to finish nursing school, hoping somehow I could eventually go after my dream of singing professionally. That never happened and I settled into my new life as a nursing student. It was the most demanding and difficult thing I had ever done in my life, and then some.

My school had very strict rules for freshmen. We were only allowed overnight leave one weekend a month, even if we lived close by. Sunday through Thursday, we had to be in the dorm by 6 p.m. Friday and Saturday we had to be in the dorm by 10 p.m. If you missed any curfew, you would lose your next overnight weekend, and have to stay at the dorm. Each room had two twin beds and two desks. Mandatory study time was from 7-9 p.m. and we had to be at our desks, never on the bed, and with the door open. You could not leave your room during these hours except to go to the bathroom. The elderly house mothers, Mrs. Rothrum and Mrs. Weaver, would continually check on us looking into each room. You rarely saw them smile. It reminded me of mom, wanting to maintain distance from human compassion. They had their own apartments on the first floor. One was always there. Sunday through Thursday, it was lights out at 10 p.m., no exception. I can still hear Ms.

Rothrum hollering down the hallway to turn off our lights as soon as the clock struck 10. Lights out was a rule for the freshmen, only.

At 9 p.m. on Monday thru Thursday, we had what we called the "milk run." The hospital dietary department would deliver cartons of chocolate and regular milk and loaves of bread and butter to our kitchen. As soon as 9 p.m. arrived, we would all make a mad dash to the kitchen trying to get there first for the chocolate milk. There was never enough chocolate milk. We would have milk and buttered toast. This comradery was new to me and a great end to our strict hours of studying. I loved living with all of the other girls. It was like one big slumber party. I was never allowed to have friends spend the night when I was growing up. I could go to their home for the night, but mom wouldn't allow me to have friends over for the night. Or maybe I didn't want to ask fearing she might embarrass me. I truly don't remember which it was. At my nursing school dorm, we went to each other's rooms to fix our hair, try on each other's clothes and talk about our boyfriends and all those things girls love to do. Warm memories.

Sparks Memorial Hospital was directly across the street from the nursing school and dormitory. The school was a beautiful red brick colonial style 3 story building with large trees in the front. Freshmen on the first floor, juniors and seniors were on the second and third floors. There was also a small attic-like fourth floor with a kitchen and a large room with tables. Our uniforms were laundered by the hospital and brought to this room once a week. The tables were piled high with stacks and stacks of uniforms for almost 100 students. There was no air conditioning in our dorm rooms or in this fourth floor area. If you were on uniform duty you had to sort these large stacks into individual student bundles and I know the temperature in that room in the summer must have exceeded 110 degrees. Our uniforms consisted of blue checked dresses and white pinafores and collars. They were starched so stiff the collars would rub blisters and calluses on our necks. We soon developed the habit of placing tissue or gauze 4 X 4s inside the collar.

Our three years were very regimented. Our first week as a freshman, we were shown a large 3 year calendar with our names printed in a column on the left. It included hours of class time and how many hours we were required to work for the hospital. There were our lives for the next 3 years on that detailed calendar. It seemed so simple. We were required to work a certain number of unpaid hours for the hospital in order to graduate. This was part of our tuition. The total out of pocket expense for the each student was $500 for the entire 3 years. This included books, uniforms, room and board. My $500 was paid by my Miss Van Buren scholarship, therefore, you might say my nursing education was free.

These three years were very difficult for me. I was not a great student in theory and made only average grades. My grades in nursing practice were excellent, though. I passed the required quarterly NLN (National League of Nursing) exams, by the skin of my teeth. My first roommate, Nancy, wasn't so fortunate and had to leave during the first 6 months. The same thing happened with my 2nd roommate, Linda, after about a year. It was sad to say goodbye to them, because they both had always wanted be a nurse. And here I was, getting accepted at the last minute for a profession I never wanted. During these times I became more determined and began to develop a strength I never knew I had. My 3rd roommate, Kathleen, was an excellent student and we made it all the way and graduated together. I believe she is one of the reasons I made it. She had a great attitude and encouraged me. We are still good friends after 58 years

One evening after we graduated and had taken our state board examination for RN licensure, several of us were together when we found out the Director of our school, Miss Folkes, had the results. I made the call to her to find out the results. Our freshman class started out with 43 but only graduated 16. She said 15 out of 16 passed. I laughed and said "Who's the dummy?" She was quiet for a few seconds and then she said, "It was you, Juanita." I could have died right there on the spot. I was devastated and handed to phone to someone else. I had passed everything but the surgical nursing section. I remember going to work at the hospital the next day and being so embarrassed. My sister had also flunked her state nursing boards, but I don't remember if she was the only one in her class like me. I just remember thinking, how could she not pass her boards? Now I knew.

I did pass on the 2nd attempt with high marks achieving national reciprocity. That experience has helped me help others over the years. I have always believed things happen for a reason. Maybe the good Lord helped me overcome this failure and get through it in order to help others facing roadblocks in life. It was like, "Look at me, the only one in her class to flunk the nursing exam. I made it and you can too." I felt obligated to share this with anyone who was struggling. It was an embarrassing statistic that turned out to be a good thing.

TIME TO GET A JOB

After graduating from nursing school in 1963, my first husband, Gary Hickey, and I moved to Russellville, Arkansas so he could attend college there. I interviewed and got a position at the Millard-Henry Clinic as a surgical nurse and office nurse. I would report to St. Mary's Hospital surgery room early every morning, Monday through Friday. It is impossible to believe, but in those days one physician and I would perform routine surgeries with only a couple of circulating nurses and a nurse anesthetist. There was no air conditioning and it was warm in the surgical room. The window would sometimes be open. I have a memory of a fly swatter hanging on the anesthesia cylinders of gas. I know, a fly swatter is not normally in a surgical suite, but we're talking about the early 60s in a small town hospital. After surgeries were completed I would return to the office and work the rest of the day.

One day a patient, who was a registered nurse, came into the office. She told me she was quitting her job as director of nursing at Mitchell Nursing home in Danville, Arkansas and asked if I would be interested in applying. The salary was much more than any RN nursing job in the area and it was only a 30 minute drive from Russellville. I interviewed and got the job. Hallelujah! I had never imagined making so much money. I think it was $350 a month, but I was only making $200 a month at the MH Clinic. We had so many living expenses plus my husband's college tuition was due for the next semester. We received no financial assistance from our families. It was all on me, although my husband had a part-time job for a few hours a week. We barely made it from week to week.

Mitchell's Nursing Home was a breath of fresh air and I loved it from day one. I looked forward to being there every day. I didn't know it at the time but this was the beginning of my long career in geriatrics. It was such a warm and friendly place to work. Maurine Mitchell was the administrator and her husband, Drexell, was the cook. Drexell had retired from the military where he served as a cook. I remember walking into that big bright kitchen and there he would be with a cigarette hanging out of his mouth stirring a large pot. He wore spotless white uniforms with a white cap perched on top of his head. Their kids, James and Agnes, had various duties around the facility after school hours. The Mitchells also owned the local hotel and had a cattle farm. It was a very small town and they knew everyone and everyone knew them. They were such a great family and I learned a so much from them. The nursing home wasn't just a business to them. They truly cared about the people they served. I have wonderful memories of this family.

There is one particular event that stands out in my mind. You must remember, I was a new graduate and registered nurse with all the life-saving procedures firmly ingrained in my mind. I felt like Florence Nightingale in my white uniform and cap. One day an elderly frail 90 something year old gentleman went into cardiac arrest. I rushed to his room and performed CPR and brought him back. This happened again the next morning with the same results. DNR (do not resuscitate) policies did not exist in the 60s. It was usually up to the physician to make this decision. That afternoon, I received a phone call from the small town's doctor in charge of the elderly man's care. I had met and talked with him many times when he made his rounds. He was a cantankerous but very wise old physician. He did not mince his words to me. He said "Juanita, please let him die in peace. You have accomplished nothing but fracture a rib and make his breathing very painful. Please let him die".......   I did.

Eventually, I interviewed for Director of Nursing at a facility under construction in Russellville, Arkansas, where I lived. I got the job and another big increase in pay. The owners were two brothers and part of an organization in Sallisaw, Oklahoma that owned many nursing homes in a multi-state region. It was in the early days of long term care facilities and government regulations and requirements were minimal. One of the owners,

Bernie Cheek had moved to Russellville during the construction and early phase of operation. The other brother, Barnie Cheek remained in Sallisaw, Ok., because he had a jewelry store there. One day Bernie came to me and said he was moving back to Sallisaw with his family. He asked if I thought I could manage the business without him. I immediately said yes, even though I was only 22 and so inexperienced. What else could I say? Nope, I have no idea what I am doing. Of course not. I needed this job. I just blundered my way through and apparently did most things satisfactorily.

My job title was Administrator/Director of Nursing but my duties included doing the payroll, writing dietary menus, teaching nurse's aides how to administer medications, and scheduling of all employees, to name a few. I managed the entire operation but for some reason I don't remember feeling overwhelmed. I was young and naive and the only licensed person in the building. One afternoon I walked into the nurses' station and to my utter amazement one of the medication aides was on her knees on the floor with a syringe. She had dropped an ampoule of medication and it had broken and the fluid contents had spilled onto the floor. She was trying to draw the fluid back into the syringe to administer. I froze in my tracks. Of course, I immediately explained she could not do this and why. I guess the class about sterile technique hadn't registered with her. I held a refresher class the following day. I was too inexperienced at the time to realize I was doing an impossible job. The government did, however, and long term rules and regulations changed drastically in the late 60s and early 70s.

In Russellville, in the mid-60s, there was a "facility" that was known in the community as a place to take the mentally incompetent and elderly who had no family and/or limited financial resources. The woman who ran it wore long black floor length attire and some kind of head dress resembling a nun. I would see her around town asking for donations. There were horrendous rumors about this place. I never saw the inside of any of the buildings, but from the outside, it resembled a junkyard. There were whispers of cages where the violent patients were kept. It closed about a year after I began employment at Russellville Nursing home. I am relating information about this facility because of a situation that involved one of their residents.

The Cheeks had generously offered me a bonus of $10 per patient, per month for each patient above the "break even" point of the financial operation. I can't remember the actual numbers except it added up to an extra bonus of $200- $300 to my salary each month when we stayed at full capacity. In the early 1960s that was a   huge amount of money. Therefore, admissions became very important to me. I received a call from the family of one of the residents at the facility I wrote about earlier, asking to admit their son to our facility. Like I said, admissions were important to me.   Therefore, sight unseen, I told them they could bring him that very day. When he was admitted, I was overwhelmed at his size. He was a very large 30 something year old man of American Indian decent. He was every bit of 6'5" tall and 250 pounds. The gentleman was quite lethargic and docile upon admission. I thought it was strange that he was delivered to us by a taxi.

That evening I received a call from the nurse aide in charge. I was on-call 24 hours per day, seven days per week. She told me that the new man had become belligerent and uncontrollable. When I arrived, the nurses were beside themselves and frightened. I knew right away that we could not allow the situation to continue. I called the hospital where I had worked as a surgical nurse, which was only a block away, and asked if we could bring him over to be admitted. They replied they could not take him and that he would probably have to be admitted to the Arkansas State Hospital in Little Rock. These arrangements could not be made until morning and I needed an immediate solution. I had no other choice but to call the family to come and get him. When I called, they told me they did not have a car. Now I understood the arrival by taxi. I explained the situation, told them I would bring him home and asked for instructions on how to get there. There were no cell phones or GPS back then.

My nurses put him and his belongings into my car, a small 1963 Corvair Monza.   He was so large, he had to bend and hold his head to the side to fit into my car. I remember telling him I was taking him home and it seemed to calm him down.

And, yes, I was scared out of my wits hoping he wouldn't lash out at me. My husband had an evening part time job as a plumber's helper and I couldn't get in touch with him to help me. Following the family's instructions, I started out on nice paved roads which soon turn to dirt roads with absolutely no street lighting. I got lost at one point and stopped at a pay phone at a gas station in the middle of nowhere and called the family for more instructions.

I drove for what seemed like an eternity and finally found their home. It was very dark and eerie as I went up the long stairs up to the front door. There were no lights outside and only a dim one inside the front door. Good Lord, it reminded me of the old house in the movie, "Psycho," only smaller, but just as creepy. Thank goodness the man who answered the door didn't look like Anthony Perkins. It was my passenger's father. He came out to the car and helped me get his son and his few belongings up the stairs. When we got him safely inside and as I was leaving, I expressed my apologies for not being able to keep him. He then said, "I didn't think you could," and closed the door before I could say anything. I wish he had told me that sooner. I drove away thinking, what in the world had just happened? I felt so relieved and cried all the way home. I also made a mental note to do pre-admission screenings before ever admitting another patient.

THE MOVE BACK TO MY HOMETOWN

After Gary graduated from college, we returned to my hometown, Van Buren, Arkansas. We moved our mobile home to my parent's acreage behind their home.   My mom was congenial most of the time and actually seemed happy we were going to be living there. We were ready to start a family but it wasn't happening. My gynecologist ordered all kinds of tests and I was finally diagnosed with severe endometriosis. Treatment was not successful.

About a year later, we decided to adopt an infant.   My OB/GYN physician currently had a young teenage patient wanting to place her infant up for adoption when she gave birth. We arranged for the adoption and hired an attorney. In early November of 1968, we received a beautiful infant girl. I couldn't believe I was a mom.   It was wonderful, but the joy and happiness was short-lived. The very next afternoon the birth mother's family decided they did not want to go through with the adoption and wanted the baby back. My attorney called my dad and ask him to break the news to me.   I could see the tears in my dad's eyes when he came in the door and knew immediately something was wrong.   I cried until I could no longer cry.   I packed a bag with a few of the things I had bought for her and wrapped her up in a beautiful yellow knit blanket....and we waited in a state of shock for the attorney to take her away. After they left with her, I was inconsolable.

I took a week away from work to get control of my emotions. Finally, I went back and each day got a little better.   Then one day a package came to my home. There was no return address. I opened the box and the first thing I saw was the beautiful yellow baby blanket I had wrapped the baby girl in before she was taken from me. The family of the baby girl had returned everything I had sent with her. My first thought was how could they be so cruel?   Did they feel guilty keeping these things and assume I would want them back?   It was a sad reminder of the loss. I never knew their reasoning. I came to the conclusion they had good intentions. Surely no one could be that mean.

When my physician, Dr. Sherman, discovered what had happened, he called me and was so apologetic. He said this had never happened before in his practice. He went on to say that he had just finished a meeting with all of the other doctors and they all agreed that the next birth placed for adoption would be ours if we wanted to try again. I immediately said yes. Dr. Sherman called in a few days to tell me "my" baby was due the first of April, 1969. We had begun construction on a new home half a mile from my parents' home and it would be completed before the birth. I was thrilled that I would have time to prepare and decorate the nursery. I had no idea if it would be a boy or a girl and could not have cared less. I have always believed that things happen for a reason. God didn't intend for that beautiful baby girl to be mine. He had other plans.

The first week of April passed and no baby. Dr. Sherman said she was overdue but everything was coming along just fine. Finally, on the morning of April 30, 1969, he called. He said, "You have a beautiful baby boy." He weighed 9 pounds and 15 ounces. He had actually been born three minutes before midnight on the 29th.   I called Gary and his response was "I thought I told you to tell them we didn't want another baby." He had never expressed that to me during the six months I had been decorating the nursery and buying baby things. That evening when he came home, I told him I would be going to get my baby and he could accompany me or not. He replied he would go, but I really didn't care one way or another.

Two days later it was decided that our new attorney, Finis Batchelor and his wife, would pick up our baby boy at the hospital and meet us at the pediatrician's office. Gary and I waited in Dr. Ben Cabell's office. I was so anxious waiting for their arrival. Finally, the door opened and Mrs. Batchelor walks in with my 2 day old baby boy and hands him to me. I was in love with this baby the moment I saw him. He was beautiful and so perfect. The Batchelors congratulated us and

29

left as Dr. Cabell came into the room. Ben smiled and said, "You finally have your baby." My husband spoke up and said, "Yeah, the easy way." I couldn't believe he said that. It caught Dr. Cabell off guard and he replied, "How dare you say that, after what she's been through." Gary was quiet after that. It was time to take my baby home.

Kevin Lee Hickey was the most adorable and wonderful baby boy. I took a couple week off from work to take care of him. It was absolutely two of the most wonderful weeks of my life. I hired an older lady, Mrs. Lamb, who was a friend of the family, to babysit Kevin while I was at work. She was fantastic and you could tell she adored Kevin right from the start. It was a great arrangement. We had a beautiful new home and a beautiful new baby boy. Life was good for a few years. My dad absolutely doted over Kevin. Mom was attentive, too. Mrs. Lamb would tell me that dad would drop by every day or so when he was making his deliveries, just to hold Kevin by himself for a few minutes. This baby was so special to all of the family and Gary gradually warmed up to being a father. Who could not love this adorable baby boy? When we finally received Kevin's birth certificate with our names on it, I breathed a sigh of relief. No one could ever take him away.

THE LOSS OF MY FATHER

I lost my dad when I was 28. He had a massive myocardial infarction at the age of 56. My world was crushed and the loss created a huge void in my life. I felt an unrealistic responsibility for his death. He had been helping us move into our new home when his first heart attack occurred at the age of 54. He was a healthy robust man and thought he could do anything. I did too. While he and Gary were moving a large dresser, dad collapsed in my front yard. We rushed him to the hospital. He was hospitalized and discharged within a matter of days. The doctor said it was a mild heart attack with no residual damage. He went back to work after receiving a clean bill of health, except for stomach ulcers. Throughout my life, he always had a bottle of Malanta or Gelusil everywhere imaginable for quick access. He began to suffer more and more with stomach pain and his physician suggested a partial gastrectomy. He was in so much pain he decided to go ahead with the surgery.

Within a few hours after the operation, dad had a massive MI and had to be put on life support. Early the next morning I received a call from the hospital that dad's condition was grave. I immediately called mom and we drove there but he died before we got to the hospital. When I walked into intensive care, the physician came to me and said, "He's gone." How could this be? Two days before, prior to surgery, he was so optimistic and joking about all the things he could eat once his stomach healed. He was just too young to die. I went to his bedside as they took all of the tubes from his body and then I held him for the longest time. It was devastating. He was my rock and now he was gone forever.

I couldn't accept that God had taken this wonderful father from me when I still needed him so much. I've never told this to anyone, let alone write it down. About a year after my dad's death, I was driving home from work and thinking about how much I missed him. That's when it happened. I had stopped at a 4 way stop sign. There's was a church across the intersection on the left. I drove by this church every day going to and from work. I don't know why, but I looked up. There was a beautiful cross on top of a steeple. Just above the cross was this perfectly, and I do mean perfectly, formed cloud. It was shaped exactly like a handgun! My dad had been a Colt handgun collector. It's one of those astounding and wonderful moments when you wish for someone to share it with. I will never forget it as long as I live and have leaned on that memory for strength during low periods in my life.

After dad died, mom depended on me more than ever. I'll have to admit, it was a good feeling. I would help her with the bookkeeping at the cleaners in my spare time. She hired an extra person to do dad's job of running the cleaning equipment. I was amazed how well she ran the business without him. She, too, only completed the 5th grade in school. It eventually became too much for her, though, and she sold the business in 1972. She went to work for another local cleaners but that didn't work out very well. She and dad had their way of doing things and it worked for them. When she went to work for others, the education factor came into play and she was embarrassed. She had 3 different jobs in one year and finally gave up working all together. Dad was a smart businessman and had built up a large savings account that she lived on until she was able to draw social security. There was also dad's life insurance and the sale of his Colt handgun collection. She managed quite well.

LIFE AND CAREER GOES ON

I became DON (Director of Nursing) and administrator of a Fort Smith nursing home in 1970. Again, I made an excellent salary and was good at my job. Before very long, though, the laws regulating nursing homes changed, requiring Administrator and DON to be separate positions. Current Administrators with less than 2 years' experience on the job were required to enroll in classes and take an exam for licensure. I took the course and got my administrator license, but a new person was hired as Administrator and I became just the DON. My salary remained the same and I continued to enjoy my work. Still there was that ever nagging and persistent desire to build my own nursing home in Van Buren and provide unique and exceptional care like the Mitchell's home in Danville. It was my dream.

After working at there for a few years, I began working on floor plans and income projections at home in the evenings, until I came up with a good presentation. The floor plans were crude, but the income projections along with anticipated expenses were derived from the valuable experience I received at Russellville Nursing Home. When the owners of the nursing home heard the whispers that I had intentions of building my own nursing home, they were upset. They came to see me at my office to verify if the rumors were true. I told them it was true, but also that I no concrete plans in place. Eventually, the situation became a strain on everyone and I gave my notice and left.

About 2-3 months after I left my employer, I received a call from Dr. Mitchell, one of the owners of it. He had a job offer for me. He had recently opened a new facility in Rogers, Ark and was in a dilemma. The administrator they had hired was very old and having episodes of dementia. He asked if I would consider replacing him and that they were open to my thoughts on a salary. Rogers, Arkansas was about a 2 hour drive north of my home. I told him I would consider it and let him know the next day. I talked to my husband that evening and said I really didn't want to take it. Dr. Mitchell had not been very kind to me during my last days at the facility and that was still on my mind. I was doing private duty nursing during the day and continued to work on plans for my own facility in the evening.

I got to thinking about his comment they were "open" to my thoughts on salary. Lord knows, I needed the money. I decided to start off with a ridiculous amount and maybe we could meet somewhere in the middle and that would take care of travel expenses. I called Dr. Mitchell and gave him my demands. I wanted a monthly salary of $4000 a month and would work four days a week.......no pause or counter offer! He immediately agreed and asked how soon I could meet him there. Good grief! You could have knocked me over with a feather! My salary at the facility had only been about $900 a month when I left. A Nursing Home Administrator salary of $4000 a month in the mid-1970s was, not only ridiculous, but unheard of.

Very early the next day, I drove to Rogers. Dr. Mitchell had his own airplane and flew from Oklahoma to Rogers to meet me. When I arrived, I walked into the building and was greeted by Dr. Mitchell. We immediately went to the office. There sat this elderly gentleman in his pajamas at the desk. He also lived at the nursing home. Licensed administrators were hard to find. Some administrators with years of experience on the job were grandfathered into the system in 1971 without taking the licensure exam. Sadly, this gentleman was one of them. I'll never forget Dr. Mitchell's comments to this poor gentleman as he introduced me. He said, "This is Mrs. Hickey and she is here to replace you." Then he turned, walked out the door and left for the airport. Did he really just do that? I stood there exasperated at his departure, but I don't think it registered at all with the pajama clad man. I went to find the DON who was the next person in charge. She related to me how bad the situation had become. I contacted his family and made arrangements for them to come and get him.

I loved my new position and my hours. I would drive to Rogers early Monday, spend the night at the nursing home and return home late Tuesday. I would stay home Wednesdays then drive up on Thursday and return home Friday evening. This was my usual schedule. They would call me on Wednesdays if problems arose, but the DON was very efficient and this rarely happened. Only one wing was occupied at the time and I spent Monday and Thursday nights in a room in the vacant wing. A couple of times during the summer, I brought my son, Kevin, and one of his friends and my godson, Darren, with me. They loved it. They rode their big wheels up and down the vacant hallway but most of all they looked forward to their early morning breakfast at IHOP on the way there.

In the meantime, I was making a lot of progress planning my own facility. I was making more money than I ever had in my life and could now afford to have an architect draw the plans. I approached mom and two other investors with the idea of building a nursing home in Van Buren. I had no money to invest, but I did have the knowledge and the know-how. I now had the architectural plans, a state CON (certificate of need) approval for a 58 bed facility, income and expense projections and investors. It was time to apply for financing and I was so excited.

We were approved within a matter of weeks. I couldn't believe it. This was the beginning of Brownwood Manor, Inc., which opened on August 31, 1974. The owners were my husband and myself, my mom, a local accountant and a doctor. It was named for my father, Buster Brown Smith. I thought Brown had a nice sound and the building site was a country setting with nothing visible but land and trees. The town soon grew out that way, though. Today, there are houses on all sides of the nursing home.

Dad's family had gotten his name from the old Buster Brown Shoes, which were popular in 1916 when my dad was born. My grandfather and grandmother's last names were Smith before they married. There was a catchy cartoon shoe commercial, at the time, about a boy, Buster Brown and his dog, Tige, who lived in a shoe. One of my grandfather's friends suffered from dwarfism and toured with the shoe company as one of their mascots, dressed in the well-known Buster Brown suit and hat. My dad said his father had told him this friend was present when dad was born. Dad never used his middle name and few people knew it. He was just Buster Smith, who owned Buster Smith Cleaners, to everyone. When Brownwood Manor, Inc. opened, the local newspaper ran an article and picture of my dad and how the nursing home was named after him. He would have been so proud.

I left my employment in Rogers approximately 9 months after I arrived. I left on good terms with the owners. I worked hard for those 9 months, increasing the census to 100 percent and hired a newly licensed administrator as my replacement and trained her before I left. There was a small local facility that was closing. I met with the owner and made arrangements to have his residents moved to there. This is what enabled me to reach 100 percent occupancy as soon as I did. I was handsomely paid, probably more than I should have been, but I did a good job and that is what mattered to me.

HOW I MET BILL CLINTON

Finally, I was managing my own nursing home. It was a thrill to go to work every day, but also difficult in the beginning. The income did not cover all the bills and payroll for the first six months. I had to get an additional loan for startup costs but things finally evened out after a while. It was close to a year before I could start paying small monthly dividends to the stockholders. I was on a salary, but the added income was great. I was the administrator and hired a Director of Nursing, Food Service Supervisor, Housekeeping and Laundry Supervisor, Activity Coordinator and Licensed Practical Nurses around the clock. It was a good operation and within a year we were at capacity with 58 residents and a waiting list.

The stockholders decided it was time to think about expanding. A 41-bed wing was added in 1976 bringing the total beds to 99. A few years later, we added a 10-bed wing of private suites with a beautiful lobby for the families and residents to visit with big screen TV, aquarium and beautiful furnishings. We also enlarged the kitchen and dining room and added a large physical therapy room. The 10 private room suites addition was built out through the front of the building on piers with a drive thru underneath. We had the first elevator in Van Buren until Citizens Bank built their new building a year or so later. Brownwood developed a good reputation and always had a waiting list. We did minimal advertising, because word of mouth was the best advertisement we had going for us.

In 1978, I was very active in community and state organizations. I was president of my district's Nursing Home Association, a member of the Board of Directors of the Arkansas Nursing Home Association, a member of the Van Buren Women's League and Chamber of Commerce. It was at this time, I began to hear about a candidate running for

Governor of Arkansas, Bill Clinton. I was invited to attend a Crawford County meeting wanting to sign people up as volunteers for his campaign. I had never been involved in politics and thought it would be interesting. I signed up as a volunteer and loaded up my nursing home van with yard signs, window signs, bumper stickers, buttons, etc., and was excited about participating in my first ever campaign. I would make calls to people I knew and didn't know who had a good spot for a yard sign. I would go around in the evenings and hand out yard signs to individuals and window signs to businesses.

About a month or so after I began volunteering, I had a call from the state campaign headquarters. Mr. Clinton was going to be on a campaign tour in the Van Buren and Fort Smith area and they wanted to know if he could come by Brownwood Manor and visit with the residents and employees. I was very excited and told them we would love to have him come by. It was scheduled. We alerted the media, the families of the residents, and others in the community who wanted to meet the candidate. We were all excited waiting for the day Bill Clinton would come to Brownwood.

It was late March or early April 1978 when Bill Clinton came to Brownwood Manor. He came in with his entourage and started shaking hands with everyone. The local newspaper asked for a group photo of myself, two residents and Mr. Clinton. He shook my hand and I immediately noticed how friendly and charismatic he was. When he talked to you he never looked away, always keeping eye contact and smiling. I had watched his news conferences and campaign ads on television and thought they were impressive. After several photos were taken, he came over to me and started asking questions about me and my nursing home.

As we spoke, I seemed to have his full attention and so I began to tell him about the problems we were having with the state reimbursement, not being enough to provide adequate care for our residents. He seemed very interested in what I saying and that he would like to have an opportunity to talk to me at length about my concerns. He then asked if I was ever in Little Rock. I said yes and that I would be attending a nursing home seminar there in a few weeks. He said for me to call his campaign headquarters when I got there and he would try to visit with me while I was there. Wow, this was exciting. Being able to talk to someone, who more than likely would be our next governor, was so encouraging. I was overwhelmed he actually wanted to speak to me one-on-one. I started working on graphs showing the monthly per-diem paid by state compared to the actual cost of providing care. I completed my presentation and was looking forward to our meeting.

It was April 24, 1978. The Director of Nursing, Norma Rogers, and I left after work for Little Rock and checked into the Camelot Hotel when we arrived. The nursing home seminar was scheduled for the next morning. We went to dinner and then retired to our room. The next morning, I called Bill Clinton's campaign headquarters. A young woman answered and I told her who I was and asked if Mr. Clinton was available. She said "No, Mrs. Hickey, but Mr. Clinton said if you ever called to ask you to call his apartment." She gave me the number and I called. Bill Clinton answered. I asked if he was going to be at his campaign office at noon so we could come over on our lunch break. He said no, but could I meet with him now. I replied that I would drive to the campaign office right away. He then said he would just come to the coffee shop of the hotel where I was. He said he would call when he arrived. I was surprised he would make that effort and thought this was absolutely awesome. I told Norma to go on to the meeting and as soon as I finished at the coffee shop, I would join her. She left and I waited in the room for his call.

The phone rang a short time later. It was Bill Clinton and he said, "There are so many people and reporters in the coffee shop. Can we just meet in your room?" I remember being a little taken aback by this request, but I believed him. He was the Attorney General and I wasn't afraid of being alone with him. I told him I would order coffee to the room and he said he was talking with someone and would be up in about 30 minutes.

There was a knock on the door within seconds after room service left. I have often wondered if he had waited for room service to leave so he wouldn't be seen. I opened the door and there he stood, with his sunglasses on. I thought that was rather strange. He came in and I ushered him to the table where the coffee was sitting along with my file of information. He was very pleasant and I began to pour each of us a cup of coffee that we never drank. From my window was a view of the river and some buildings. He took off his suit coat and laid it over the chair. He didn't have on a tie, just a white shirt with the top button unbuttoned. He began to talk and point to something below. He said it was an old jail house from the 1800s and when he became Governor he wanted to restore it to its original condition. I walked over to where he was standing to see what he was talking about. The next thing I knew he put his arm around my shoulder while he was pointing to the building. Instantly, this made me extremely uneasy. Then all of a sudden he turned me toward him and began to kiss me. I was flabbergasted.

I immediately backed away from him and said something to the effect of "Wait a minute, I am married." He pulled me back to him. Again I pulled away and I told him, "I am married......and I also other things going on in my life." My husband wasn't the real main reason I wanted nothing to do with Bill Clinton. I was married, but my marriage was on the rocks, and I had been having an affair with another man. I was deeply in love with this man and had no desire to be with Bill Clinton other than professionally. At this point, he grabbed me again and this time I realized that he wasn't taking no for an answer. He pushed me backwards onto the bed and I began to panic and yell. Then he was on top of me biting my lip. It was a shock and so painful. I began to taste the blood from my bleeding lip and I was so frightened. His hands were all over me. He tore at my clothes, ripping my skirt at the waist. He was so heavy and I thought I wasn't going to be able to get my breath. He would bite my lip if I started to yell and then he would press down on my shoulder with one elbow while he tore at my clothes with his free hand. I truly thought I was going to die.

He pushed my skirt up and tried to pull my panty hose down. They were the sheer kind and began to rip with his repeated yanks. I never wore underwear under my panty hose. This is one time I wished I had. He ripped my panty hose completely away from the crotch area. I don't remember him undoing his pants. All of a sudden I just felt his bare skin against mine.

And then the rape began and it was so painful that I screamed. That's when the lip biting commenced again to quiet me. As long as I remained quiet, he would not bite me. At one point I remember thinking, dear God, please let it be over soon. In a few minutes, it was over and he stopped moving. He just laid on top of me and I wanted him to get off. I was crying by then and still he just laid there on top of me. I could hardly breathe. After 10 or 15 seconds I heard him mumble "I'm going to do it again." He started moving again and it was over in about a minute or less. Then he finally rolled off of me. Thank goodness, I could finally get a good breath.

I sat up on the side of the bed pulling the cover around my waist and legs. By this time, I was sobbing uncontrollably. He didn't say anything while he straightened himself and put on his suit coat. He just stood there looking at me with an expression that's hard to describe. It was a cross between bewilderment and frustration. Then he said, "I'm sterile. I had mumps when I was a kid." I wanted to say, "You've just raped me and that is what you have to say!" But all I could do was cry. Then he walked to the door, calmly put on his sunglasses and turned to me and said, "You'd better put some ice on that" and walked out the door. The entire encounter was less than an hour but it changed my life forever.

What in God's name had just happened? I was brutally raped, my lip was throbbing and hurting as well as other parts of my body, and I was frightened to death. I had this overwhelming feeling that someone might come in to get rid of the "body." That's what I felt like, a body. I went to the door and locked it and went back to the bed and laid down. I didn't want to move or look in the mirror at the injuries. I must have laid there an hour or more before I heard a knock at the door. When I looked through the peephole, I saw Norma. Dear God, I had completely forgotten about her and the seminar. I had just wanted to go to sleep and wake up from this bad dream. When I opened the door and saw the look on her face, I started crying all over again.

I will never forget how attentive Norma was to me as I began to tell her what had happened. She was not just my employee. She was a dear friend and I will be forever in her debt. Being a nurse, she immediately got ice for my mouth. She asked what I wanted to do and I said I just want to go home. She helped me change my clothes and then she packed all of our belongings and we headed for Van Buren. By the time we left the hotel, the bleeding had stopped, but my lip was swelling. Luckily, on the way out of the hotel, we didn't meet anyone we knew and didn't have to explain our early departure or my appearance. I don't remember much about the drive home except for Norma stopping a couple of times to get ice for my lip.

By the time I got home, I had arrived at the decision not to tell my husband what had happened. I thought about it all the way home. I was already blaming myself for allowing Bill Clinton to come to my room and knew my husband would do the same. As I said before, our marriage was not good and most likely headed for divorce. So how did I explain my lip injury? I told him I had been hit in the mouth by a revolving door. I truly don't remember his reaction. We had come to the point in our marriage where we rarely spoke to one another unless it was necessary. We divorced a few months later. I can't remember my son, Kevin, knowing or asking about my lip. I do remember being in a daze trying to get ready for his birthday on the April 29, 1978. He was having a skating party for his ninth birthday.

I saw David Broaddrick, the man I was having an affair with, a day or two after the rape. My lip was not as swollen after about 48 hours and only showed bruising on the outside and make up helped to hide the discoloration. Inside my lip were blood blisters and sores like when you accidentally bite the inside of your cheek. It was so sore. There was no make up to hide my wounded spirit, though. I was a different person and David knew it. I finally broke down and told him. He was beside himself with rage. I was afraid he would try to do something to Bill Clinton and reminded him we were talking about the Attorney General of Arkansas.

A few days after the rape, I decided to get rid of all of the Clinton campaign items I had been carrying around in the nursing home van. There was a business in Van Buren called Kay Chair Company. Every evening they would burn all the wood and material scraps from that day. The fire was in an area behind their business that was contained but accessible to the public. I backed the van up a safe distance from the fire and yes, I began to toss all of the Clinton yard sign, bumper stickers, window signs, hats, t-shirts, etc., into the fire. It felt so good to see the Bill Clinton name burning and disappearing. The buttons wouldn't burn so I put them in a plastic bag and threw them in the dumpster at the nursing home.

There were others I told about the rape in the following days including Norma's sister, Jean Darden, who was the Assistant Director of Nursing and also a close friend. Norma and I told her, but I cannot recall how soon it was after we returned from Little Rock. Susan (Beckham) Lewis was a close friend and I was the Godmother of her children. She called me one day and said she needed to talk to me in private away from our families. It was within days after the rape. We met at the city park. She started by saying there were rumors going around town about me. I was taken completely off guard and thought, "Oh my God, she knows about Clinton." I think I said. "Who told you about Bill Clinton?" I assumed she had found out what happened in Little Rock. She looked at me like I was crazy and asked, "Bill Clinton?" Instead, she had wanted to warn me about the rumors going around about my relationship with David Broaddrick. I had not wanted to burden Susan with this, but had no choice except to tell her about the rape. I also told Kathleen Emerson Crigler and Louise Ma, both friends from nursing school.

MEETING HILLARY CLINTON

I knew there was a campaign fundraiser for Bill Clinton in two to three weeks at Dr. Buddy Crisswell's home in Van Buren, because I had helped organize it. People would come from the state campaign office to bring supplies and meet with us every week or so. I told a state volunteer on one of their trips to Van Buren I couldn't volunteer anymore, because my business was demanding too much of my time. If only I could have told her they were working to elect a rapist. I also told her I couldn't attend the fundraiser event.

The day before the fundraiser, my assistant administrator, Berta Young, brought me an envelope. Another employee who had driven the van that day found the envelope and brought it to her. It contained a few checks, each amounting to $25 or less and written to the Clinton campaign. They had been given to me by people in the community when I delivered their yard signs. I had completely forgotten about them when I was cleaning out the van. I called the state campaign office to see where to send them. I was told that a lady from their office was going to be at the fundraiser the next evening in Van Buren and would I please give them to her.

I decided I would go, give her the checks, make an appearance and then leave. Dr. Crisswell and his wife, Betty were good friends and excited about having this event in their home. They were unaware of what Bill Clinton had done. Betty and I were both tennis players at the same club, and her husband, Dr. Crisswell, was my dentist. I went early before the event to meet with the woman from the state office. A funny side note to this is when I met her, I thought she was Bill Clinton's mother. She looked like her. I was told later that she was not his mother. I was talking to someone when Chuck Watts, a local pharmacist and friend, came over to me. He was excited. He did not know about the rape and was a huge Clinton supporter. He had driven the Clintons from the airport to the Crisswell home and began telling me that the topic of the conversation all the way from the airport in Fort Smith (about 20 minutes) was about me. I froze.

As soon as Chuck finished talking, I saw the Clintons coming through the back kitchen area. I panicked and tried to leave, but they were between me and the front door. I realized coming here had been a huge mistake. I saw someone talking to Hillary and pointing to me and here she came, straight for me. I remember thinking, "Oh my Lord, here comes this poor woman married to such an evil man." Hold that thought. She walked directly to me smiling and said, "I just want you to know how much Bill and I appreciate everything you do for his campaign." Good Lord, what do I do now? I said something like "Thank you," and started to walk to the door. Then all of a sudden someone grabs my arm. I thought it was someone behind me at first, but as I turn around, I see that it's Hillary who had hold of me. Her smile had faded and instead there was a very angry scowl to replace it. She had a strong grip on my hand and arm. She pulled me close to her and said in a low threatening voice, "Do you understand? Everything you do," with the emphasis on 'everything.' Did she just say that? Was that a threat? I definitely took it as one. I jerked free from her grip and left, immediately.

Good heavenly days, I thought on the way home. Did Hillary Clinton know what her husband had done to me and did she just threaten me to keep quiet? What else could I think after that encounter? Why would she protect him? Why would she stay married to such a despicable man? Years later we would find out why. She went through all the personal humiliation for her own political aspirations. She has never been a true advocate for women's rights. She is and always has been an advocate for one woman......Hillary Clinton.

During the next few months after the rape, I would get phone calls at my office from Bill Clinton. When he called the first two or three times, I told my assistant, Berta Young, to tell him I was not there or unavailable. This was uncomfortable because she would have a look of surprise on her face, wondering why I didn't want to talk the Arkansas AG who was probably going to be the next Governor. Unfortunately, one day I was answering the phone while my assistant was at lunch. When I answered in the usual greeting, "Brownwood Manor, Mrs. Hickey, where can I direct your call," the voice on the other end responded, "Hi, it's Bill. When are you coming to Little Rock again?" I think I said, "I'm not," and hung up, but I could have just hung up. How could he be so arrogant and think I would ever want anything to do with him, again? I couldn't believe it. It was disgusting. He never called me again.

DIVORCE AND AN OUT OF CONTROL HUSBAND

There was a very unfortunate occurrence with my husband, Gary Hickey. I filed for divorce and moved Kevin and I into a new home in Van Buren. Gary suspected and eventually found out about David and was angry. When I left the marriage, I had no plans to marry David. I just wanted my unhappy marriage to end and make a new life for Kevin and me. We had been in our new home for approximately a week. Kevin had two little boys over to spend the night. The boys were in Kevin's room and I was watching TV in my bedroom. It was probably 8 or 9 p.m. on Friday or Saturday night.

I heard pounding on my bedroom wall coming from the back yard. Then, the yelling started, but I had no idea who it was. I went to Kevin's room and told the boys to shut and lock the door and stay in the room. I then proceeded to the kitchen to call the police. Before I could get there, the entire front door came crashing in and ended up lying in the entryway. As he walked over the door, I could see it was Gary and he had a gun. I later found out it was a 30-30 rifle. He was screaming David's name saying he was going to kill him and started down the hall. Of course, David wasn't there. I was afraid for the boys and tried to stop him. He hit me with the butt of the rifle he was carrying and knocked me to the floor. I was bleeding and felt my nose was broken. (In 99 media said my injuries from 4-25-78 were probably from my husband because they had found the police report on this incident which happened months after the rape). Gary was mean spirited, but he had never hit me before that night.

After Gary realized David was not there, he broke the door on Kevin's room and grabbed him by the arm and drug him down the hall and out the gaping hole where the front door had been. I was dazed, bleeding profusely from my nose as I ran after them. It was too late. I watched Gary drive away with my son. I ran to Kevin's room to make sure the other little boys were okay. I tried to stay calm for their sake, but seeing me in my condition did not help to calm them. My nightgown was soaked down the front in blood. They were frightened and I told them to come with me to the kitchen while I called for help. I grabbed a robe and put it on to hide all the blood. I couldn't think straight.

I called my friend, Jean Darden, and her husband, Dr. Darden. They lived only a few blocks away and came immediately. They called the parents of the boys and the police. My main concern was Kevin. I was beside myself with worry about what Gary might do to him. He had a drinking problem but had never done anything like this before. The police assured me that would begin searching immediately for him and I heard them call in to dispatch with description of the car and its occupants....and also that Gary had a gun. Apologies were made to the boys' families when they came to pick them up. I was so embarrassed. The builder I had bought the house from came over and covered the front door with plywood. I called mom to make arrangements to spend the night at her home and told the police where I would be. Doc and Jean went home and I drove to mom's house.

Early the next morning, my divorce attorney called and said that Gary has contacted him and Kevin was just fine. He also said Gary knew the police were looking for him and he would return Kevin if I would drop any charges against him. I told him to tell him yes, I would drop the charges, but also he would have to sell his shares of stock in Brownwood Manor to me. I was surprised he agreed to the stock sale because I would not have insisted on it in order to get Kevin back home, safely. Everything was agreed upon in writing and within an hour I had my baby back. (The stock sale became a part of the divorce decree and this will become important later in my story)

My son had been through a lot and I just wanted things to calm down and get back to as normal as could be under the circumstances. I didn't see David for a month or so. I just wanted to concentrate on my son, who was the single most important thing in my life. Kevin finally told me his dad drove to the Arkansas River bottoms after they left my house and slept in the car. Can you imagine what was going through his young mind seeing his mother injured and bloody while he was being dragged out of his home by a raving maniac of a father? How could a loving father do this to his child? There was no excuse for what he did to Kevin and he has never given me a reason to forgive him for it.

After several weeks, I began to see David again. I thought Kevin was a doing good and it was time for things to get back to normal. I wanted that to include David and his family. Apparently, I was wrong about my son's adjustment. About a year after he was dragged out into the night by his father, I received a phone call from his teacher, Beverly Watts. She was the wife of Chuck Watts, the friend who had driven the Clintons to the fundraiser. She said she was concerned about Kevin and related an incident that happened that day after a lunch or recess break. All of the students were back in the classroom except for Kevin. When she looked in the hallway, he was there and he was crying.

She went over to him to ask why he was crying. Kevin told Mrs. Watts he was afraid his daddy was going to hurt his mom. I was completely overwhelmed with shame. Why hadn't I picked up on this? I truly thought he was adjusting well to our new life and all of that was behind us. I told her about the situation because I felt she needed to know. I thanked her for calling me and asked if she would please keep me informed of anything else that might come up.

That evening I talked to Kevin about what Mrs. Watts had told me. He was only 10 and seemed embarrassed about it, not really wanting to talk about it. I assured him that things were fine between his dad and me and not to worry about his dad hurting me. He truly did not want to talk about it. We did have a few unfortunate situations in the early months following the divorce. Gary's visitation with Kevin was every other weekend and every Wednesday evening for a few hours. On Wednesday evenings, Kevin would get ready and wait, looking out the front window. Many of those evenings, his dad would never call or show up. It was sad to see him looking out the window and watching for his dad. Again, how could Gary be so cruel? I finally told Gary that if this happened again, I would speak with my attorney about discontinuing the Wednesday evening visitation.

One morning while Kevin was at his dad's for the weekend, he called me very early and said he and his dad were supposed to go hunting and his dad was still asleep. I told him to just go in and wake him. His reply broke my heart. He said, "I don't want to. I'm afraid of him." I tried not to be alarmed and told him not to hang up and to lay the phone down and go wake his dad. He did just that and came back to the phone and very happily announced, "It's okay mom, dad's awake and we're going hunting." He hung up the phone before I could say anything.

STARTING OVER AGAIN

Things improved dramatically over the next several months when Gary started dating a lovely young woman named Dana. When Gary was out of town or unable to get Kevin on Wednesdays, Dana would pick him up and take him to eat or take him to the video games arcade or to the movies. She was delightful and so young, in her very early twenties. One Wednesday evening, when Dana brought Kevin home, he came in the door and said, "Mom, can Dana come in for a while?" I was caught off guard, but I said sure she can. I was in my bathrobe, ironing and had a towel wrapped around my freshly washed hair but I didn't care. I chuckled as he excitedly went to get her. She visited with us for a while and Kevin was so happy. I was glad he had this kind, young woman in his life who seemed to genuinely care for him. Dana's parents became wonderful grandparents to Kevin after she and Gary married a year or so later.

David and I were getting closer and one evening he asked me to marry him. I accepted. This would be the second marriage for both of us. David had two boys and it was important to us to make sure all of the boys, including Kevin, were ready for this next step. Kevin really liked David and I knew he would be a great step-father. David and Kevin are close to this day.

We were married one evening in February, 1981, in Crested Butte, Colorado. We both loved to snow ski and thought we could get married and have a great ski trip at the same time. We were married in the city courthouse by a municipal judge after he finished court. Our witnesses were the local sheriff and his deputy who happened to be there for a case.

My mother considered David an opportunist and didn't like him. I was financially secure and owned a nursing home and he was a plumber/pipe fitter that was unemployed some of the time. He was respectful to her, but I know it hurt him when he would hear critical remarks she would make about him to anyone who would listen. I would become angry but he would always be the person to calm any situation that arose from her comments.

Early on I made a position for mom at Brownwood and paid her a small salary, hoping this would appease her. She would come to the nursing home every day but really just be there, talking to residents and their families. This was a huge mistake. After David and I married, she would go to the employees break room and make her disapproval of David well known. One day, a very loyal employee came to me and said mom was making horrible comments about me. This was so hurtful. As soon as I would hear about her negative remarks, I would call her in my office and confront her. She would lie and say she never said it, but I knew she did. It would get better for a while but then it would happen over and over again causing temporary employee turmoil. Employees soon learned the character of my mother and instead of coming to me, they ignored her. Families of residents would say to me, "I just love your mom and you are so lucky to have her here with you." I would cringe and say thank you.

Why did I put up with my mother? Here's my answer. Brownwood Manor was my dream and I was not going to let her take that away from me. All she had done was invest $25K, which had been paid back within the first two years. I had given my everything to make Brownwood a reality. I owned 25 %(after I purchased Gary's 12.5 %), mom owned 25% and the other 50% was owned by the doctor and accountant. They had become disgruntled over the dividends I was able to pay each month. The regulations were requiring more staffing of professional as well as minimum wage employees and inflation was killing us. This is my reason for meeting with Bill Clinton 3 years earlier. I refused to cut back on the food and care to the bare minimum requirements. I was a nurse first and a business woman second. It was important to me to provide the best possible care without going in the red. I knew the time would come when we could provide good care and make a profit, too. The way the corporation was set up, I was in control. I couldn't be replaced as administrator and business manager without a majority vote of stockholders. I knew if I made mom unhappy, she might side with the others and I would still be an owner but out of a job. I had to handle her with kid gloves and swallow my pride many times to keep her happy.

After the divorce, my ex-husband, Gary, refused to sell his shares to me. I had to eventually file a lawsuit against him demanding he surrender his stock. I testified first and then Gary. Then to my surprise the Brownwood Manor owner/accountant appeared and testified on Gary's behalf hoping to have the stock purchase agreement nullified. He was wanting to purchase Gary's stock. Gary got on the witness stand and lied through his teeth. He said he never hit me and the gun was not loaded. He further testified that he was blackmailed into signing the divorce decree which included the stock sale.

In my talks with Kevin, after his father broke into our home, he told me he saw his dad take the bullets out of the gun. I always remembered that. The lady judge would have nothing to do with Gary's story. She had the divorce decree and the police report in front of her. She ruled as soon as the accountant finished his testimony. She spoke directly to me and asked, "Mrs. Broaddrick, do you have the finances to purchase Mr. Hickey's stock?" I replied, "Yes, your honor, I do." She then ordered Gary to surrender his stock to me that day. This chapter was over and I had won. I wanted to hug her.

I was so angry at the underhanded way the accountant had testified on Gary's behalf. Monthly Board of Director meetings became very strained after that very public backstabbing. The doctor and the accountant finally realized that I was not going to cut back on patient care expenses in order to increase dividends. Mom was drawing a salary and was satisfied. The doctor was our Medical Director and drew a salary for that position plus his office billed Medicare/Medicaid for monthly patient visits. The accountant drew a salary for doing our bookkeeping and cost reports to the state. They were both difficult to deal with in the day to day operation of

Brownwood. I fired both of them. They balked but I was management and until they could get a majority vote of stockholders to vote otherwise, the terminations would stand. I no longer had to contend with these people anymore except at monthly corporate Board Meetings required by our articles of incorporation.

The accountant and the physician eventually sold their shares to mom and me in the 90s and we each ended up with 50%. Now, she could do nothing to hurt me financially. I was in control. I called her into my office and told her if I ever heard another negative word about me or David, I would fire her. She would remain an owner but would not be employed and draw a salary. This was the end of our relationship for many years. She finally quit coming to the nursing home altogether after her driver's license was revoked due to severe macular degeneration. She sold her shares to me in 2005 and I became the sole owner.

BROWNWOOD LIFE CARE CENTER

In late 1986 or early 1987, David and I became aware that the old Sparks Manor building in Fort Smith was for sale. It was built in the mid-1950s as an exclusive nursing home for wealthier clientele. It was all private rooms and owned and managed by Sparks Hospital. I started doing research on what was needed in the area that this building would accommodate. I contacted Arkansas Department of Human Services and was informed we could not get a certificate of need for nursing home beds, but that there was a need for ICFMR (Intermediate Care Facility for Mentally Retarded) beds. A children's ICFMR facility in Clarksville, Arkansas was closing and there would be beds available for a CON application.

Brownwood Manor stockholders, except for the physician, decided to buy the building. Sparks Hospital carried the loan with no down payment. It was closed as a retirement facility in the early 80s due to being a financial drain on the hospital. It was a then turned into a drug rehab unit as well as other services but eventually it was closed and sat empty. When we took over as owners, it was inhabited by a few homeless people who had broken in. I wondered if they had been there as patients in the drug program.

Sparks Manor was in disrepair and required a lot of painting and minor repairs. A lot of the furnishings were included in the sale of the building. It was a fantastic location near Sparks Hospital in downtown Fort Smith on 13 acres. It was much larger than Brownwood Manor and we only needed space to care for 50 children. This building was extravagantly built, having huge lobbies, offices, library, large kitchen and dining room, including an employee dining and break room, physical therapy room. I remember working there as DON and as a nursing student and thinking about how awesome it would be to own a facility in a building like this. This became a reality as Brownwood Life Care Center.

We got a CON (certificate of need) for 50 beds from the state and began the transfer of approximately 30 of the children from an ICFMR facility in Clarksville that was closing. All of the children at that facility did not come to Brownwood and were moved to other facilities closer to their families. This was a great start for operating capital. We were in business. I hired an administrator to manage Brownwood Manor nursing home and became administrator of Brownwood Life Care Center, while being a preceptor to David. He had to complete a certain number of hours of training under the direct supervision of a Licensed Administrator before he could test for his administrator license. This took about six months. I went by the nursing home every day to check on the operation there before going to work at Brownwood Life Care. This worked well.

We filled up in a very few months, taking children, even newborns with severe congenital defects, from Arkansas Children's Hospital in Little Rock. I set up an intensive care unit for the newborn infants with licensed nurses assigned around the clock to that unit. Eventually, we discontinued this unit because it did not fit into our long term care program. It required too much complex nursing care and detracted from our main objective of offering a setting for children requiring, not only cognitive behavior programs, but special education and intermediate nursing care. According to the Federal Guidelines, nursing care was not the primary function of an ICFMR. Cognitive and behavioral goals through occupational therapy, speech therapy and physical therapy and special education classes were the primary requirements of an ICFMR program.

When Brownwood Life Care first opened, a two year old girl, suffering from cerebral palsy, was admitted to our facility. Her name was Devon. The mother admitted her, left her in our care and did not return for many months. She would call but not visit in person. I felt so sorry for this child. Most of the children had families who would routinely visit. On weekends I would bring her to my home and care for her and take her back on Sunday evenings. I began to feel the strain after a month or so, essentially working 7 days a week. I was not getting any time for myself. Caring for Devon on the weekends was difficult, but I felt so guilty if I didn't because she had no family to visit her. She had a feeding tube and a number of medications and required continuous supervision. I reduced the weekends to about once or twice a month and finally not at all.

I truly loved this beautiful little girl but I had done her a disservice, not realizing I could not keep up this pace. She would cry for me when I wasn't around. At the same time, an LPN, Laura Richmond, who worked at BLCC, also loved Devon as I did. She was an exceptional nurse. I asked her to give Devon as much attention as possible because I was going to reduce my time with her. I felt guilty, but I had no choice. I looked in on her one day, after I hadn't seen her in a few weeks and she saw me and began to cry. It broke my heart and I went to her and hugged her and then I had to start the process all over again I can see why so many families are forced to place their children with severe disabilities in a facility. The care they require is continuous, 24 hours a day, seven days a week. It is exhausting and you have absolutely no time for a normal family life, especially if you have other children.

The next time I checked on her was several months later. She looked at me with a slight recognition but she didn't cry. She looked happy and I was thrilled as I left her room. David had gotten his administrators license and was doing a great job managing Brownwood Life Care with Greg Keller's guidance. I had been unable to emotionally adapt to the children's facility. I was too soft hearted and wanted to take all the children home with me. I felt sorry for them. They were not like my elderly patients who would tell me stories about their life adventures and their families. These children would never experience that. I returned to full time management at Brownwood Manor.

Early on, when my mother found out there were no dividends at the new facility, due to strict Federal guidelines, she sold her stock to the accountant and David and I. We each now had, 33

1/3 percent and the accountant was in the minority. He had set up an office on the back wing for his accounting business, rent free   in lieu of the bookkeeping fee for BLCC. David and I drew a salary. Things became strained after the accountant's assistant embezzled money from Brownwood Life Care. We prosecuted her and she went to prison.

BILL CLINTON'S APOLOGY TO ME

In the late summer or early fall of 1991, I was in North Little Rock at a nursing home seminar with Jean Darden and Norma Rogers. During the meeting a man came to the door and said I was needed outside. I went outside and Jean and Norma followed, concerned it might be some kind of emergency. The man said someone wanted to talk to me and pointed toward the end of the hallway. Norma and Jean waited while I walked in that direction. When I reached the end of the hallway, I looked around the corner and there stood Bill Clinton. He walked toward me and I was totally taken by surprise. I had not been in his presence or talked to him since 1978.

He came over to me and immediately began apologizing for what had happened the morning of April 25, 1978. He kept saying things like, "I'm a changed man, I'm a family man, I'm not the man I used to be and I am sorry for what I did to you." He just kept talking and apologizing, and then he stopped and looked at me, waiting for some kind of reply. I was shocked, but this quickly turned to anger, remembering all he had put me through and how I had blamed myself for letting him come to my room. All I could think was, you bastard, it wasn't my fault. It was your fault. I looked him straight in the eyes and said, "You go to Hell!" Then I turned and walked back to my friends. I never blamed myself again.

I told them about the encounter and later, when we went on our lunch break, we discussed it at length. Was he really sorry for what he had done to me? Did he want me to forgive him? What on earth did he want from me? Bill Clinton had just apologized for raping me. What bought this to the surface after all these years? Well, it just so happens, on October 3, 1991 he announced he was officially a candidate for President of the United States! "That's" why the profuse apology. He was trying to tie up a loose end that might throw a kink in his run for President. That's all it was. He wasn't sorry and he definitely was not a changed man. He was in damage control mode.

How could he even consider running for President of the United States. He was a rapist. It was time for me to come forward. Then, in 1992, the news of Gennifer Flowers' affair with Clinton came on the television in the lobby by the nurses' station. Norma, Jean and I looked at each other and smiled, thinking this should do it. Great day in the morning! I was so relieved. She was going to do what I had been unable to do.....bring Bill Clinton down.

Surely all the revelations she was announcing to the world would destroy this despicable human being to the point he would withdraw his candidacy. It dragged on for weeks and then Hillary did her "Tammy Wynette 'not' standing by your man" routine and women's right leaders were praising her for her courage. Oh my Lord, it wasn't courage. It was her deceitful ambition as she began her campaign to destroy Gennifer and any other woman accusing her husband sexual misconduct. She should have been up for an academy award for that performance.

I have always thought Gennifer Flowers was honest and credible. The media and tabloids did a number on her. Even the ones who had paid her handsomely for the photos and interviews seemed to turn on her. From what I have heard, she felt betrayed by them. I felt sorry for her and there was no way I was going to let that happen to me. I was so relieved I had not come forward.

In the early 90s rumors of Bill Clinton raping me would surface every now and then. David and I would ignore them or deny them. We were happy and didn't want to upset the applecart. We walked around this huge elephant (the rape) in our personal relationship denying its existence openly to each other, but it was simmering in both our minds. Then the Clintons would be in the news on television and it was a race to see who could grab the remote the quickest, to change the channel.

There were difficult times, but we seem to overcome them. David and I were members of the Episcopal Church and went to regular services at 11 a.m. This service included prayers for the President, Governor and mayor and would mention them by name. I would cringe every time Bill Clinton's name was mentioned and it became absolutely unbearable. We switched to the 8 a.m. service. This was a briefer service and the priest did not mention their names, just their title. David would squeeze my hand when he mentioned President, but not the name, Bill Clinton. One little battle won.

David did confront Clinton a few years after the rape when he accompanied me to a nursing home conference. Bill Clinton was Governor by then and the keynote speaker at the conference. When it came time for Clinton to speak, we left the meeting hall. I never wanted to be in Clinton's presence. I went to our hotel room and David returned later to say he had spoken to Clinton. This is the way he described his encounter. After Clinton's speech, David followed him to the exit and waited for his opportunity to be alone with him. He said Clinton acknowledged him, shook his hand and made a comment about him being with me. David then said, "Don't you ever go near my wife or Brownwood Manor again," squeezing Clinton's hand very hard. Clinton replied, "Listen, I never knew you were in the picture." That was a bold face lie and Clinton knew it. I had told him there was someone else before the rape. He said Clinton looked frightened and freed his hand from David's grip. It was then that Clinton's driver pulled up and the Governor made a quick exit. That's how it ended. As far as I knew they never met or spoke again.

JANE DOE #5

In 1993, I began to hear rumors about a woman named Paula Jones who was going to file a sexual harassment suit against Bill Clinton. Then on January 17, 1994, the lawsuit was filed against Clinton for $700K and Paula went public with her accusations. I never doubted her claims, knowing what he had done to me. Then the following August, Clinton's attorneys filed a motion to dismiss Jones' case citing presidential immunity. A federal judge ruled that Clinton could not stand trial until he left office. However, he ruled that the investigation into those allegations could continue. In 1996, Paula's attorneys won the right to proceed to trial in the Supreme Court and once again Clinton won another request to delay until he left office.

While looking into the various Clinton scandals, including Whitewater and the firing of the White House Travel Office staff, Independent Counsel Kenneth Star began looking into allegations that President Clinton had perjured himself and obstructed justice in the Paula Jones case. I kept thinking with each alleged scandal that broke, surely Clinton's nine lives were up. I couldn't have been more wrong. The Clintons were bulletproof. It was about this time rumors about my rape began to surface again. I would have phone calls from reporters wanting me to comment on these rumors. I would just hang up.

Sometime in 1997, two investigators hired by Paula Jones' attorneys showed up at my front door. We didn't have a security gate at our home at this time. I went to the door and there they stood. I went to the front porch to talk to them. They began to ask me about the rumors. At the time, I did not know I was being recorded. Their names were Rick and

Beverly Lambert, parents of Miranda Lambert, who became a huge country recording star years later. I told them I did not want to talk about it because it was too painful. They were very cordial and realized they were not going to get me to make any statements except it was something I did not want to talk about. They left and I assumed I had handled it satisfactorily and that would be the end of that! Man was I wrong. Things began to unravel and my name was beginning to surface more and more.

From the National Review:

The question of the affidavit is more interesting. In November 1997, Rick and Beverly Lambert, private investigators hired by Paula Jones's legal team, secretly recorded a conversation they had with Juanita Broaddrick on her doorstep in Van Buren. Broaddrick was not amenable to being interviewed, but the reasons she offered were noteworthy: "Oh, bad things, I can't even begin to tell you," she says at one point. "It's not pleasant and I won't even go into it. . . . It's very private. We're talking about something 20 years ago. . . . It's just that was a long time ago and I don't want to relive it." When the Lamberts suggest that the accusations of sexual misconduct might harm Clinton, Broaddrick says: "Well, there's just absolutely no way that anyone can get to him, he's just too vicious." 'I was afraid that I would be destroyed like so many of the other women have been.'

I was named Jane Doe # 5 in the Paula Jones case against Clinton. I decided it was time to retain legal counsel and made an appointment with Bill Walters in Greenwood, Ark. Bill and his wife, Shirley, were friends and he was also an Arkansas state senator. In the beginning, Kevin, David and I did not tell Mr. Walters I had been raped by Bill Clinton and he did not ask. We simply told him that we wanted nothing to do with the Jones case and to do whatever he could to get me removed from it.

I received the first letter from the Jones attorneys in November or December of 1997 requesting that I be deposed. The deposition took place in Bill Walters's office on January 2,

1998 and I denied all of the rumors of rape by Bill Clinton. I was determined not to let someone draw me into their lawsuit for their own personal and financial gain. I didn't know Paula at that time. I do now and respect her and believe her allegations against Bill Clinton. I had gone through years of silence and it was absolutely terrifying to realize I was now being pulled unwillingly into this case. I was truly frightened of what the Clintons might do. As long as I denied all the allegations, I would not be called. I denied the rape.

David Schippers was appointed by Henry Hyde and the Judicial Committee as lead counsel for the investigation of Bill Clinton in the impeachment process. I was to be deposed by one of Shipper's attorneys. He was accompanied by Diana Woznicki, an investigator. She was working as a Chicago Police Sergeant and took a leave of absence when she was hired by Schippers. During the interview or deposition she would watch me intently as though she felt my pain and knew I was lying and I would look away. I do not recall the exact details of how we got together after the deposition. Diana does not remember either. I do remember going to the hotel where she was staying and confessing to her at length about the rape.

In April, 1998, my attorney received a notice from the Independent Counsel's office wanting to have another interview with me. The information I had shared with Diana Woznicki was now known because I had given her permission to talk with Dave Schippers. My son, Kevin, who's an attorney, came to me and said, "Mom, this is serious. This is the Federal government and you have to tell the truth." David agreed and the three of us went to meet with my attorney, Bill Walters, to tell him the truth about the rape. I can't say it was a surprise to him. He was a Republican and did not have much use for Bill Clinton. If he thought I was lying in the Jones deposition, and the first Independent Counsel meeting, he never insinuated it. He listened intently to what Kevin was telling him: That I now needed tell the truth. Bill Walters said he would notify independent counsel and arrange the deposition.

Ken Starr did not use my deposition in the impeachment hearing. I was asked if I had ever been requested by Bill Clinton or any of his representatives to lie about any of my allegations of rape. My answer was no. I had not been asked to lie. I did that on my own out of fear of retribution. I was, therefore, no use to the impeachment hearing process because the charges were obstruction of justice.

LISA MYERS AND OTHER MEDIA

It was at this time I began to get phone messages and mail from television network correspondents and TV hosts requesting interviews with me. They included Connie Chung, Barbara Walters, Roseanne Barr, Lisa Myers and many others. I did not return any of these call or correspondence. I even had a phone message from National Enquirer offering a large sum of money for an exclusive interview. I definitely did not respond to that one. Then, Myers started contacting my son and me, trying to secure an interview. Lisa then sent me the following letter:

March 16, 1998   *NBC NEWS*

Dear Mrs. Broaddrick,

If I were you, I'd be among the last people on earth I'd want to hear from. But last night as I watched Kathleen Willey on television, I couldn't help thinking about you. Last night Willey got her story out in a highly dignified way. You now have the right moment to finally tell your story.

I also wanted to update you on where things stand for you, at least as best I can tell. Paula Jones' lawyers left your name and anything related to your story OUT of the filing which was made public Friday. Their reasoning was if they included parts of your deposition and other facts they've gathered about what happened in Little Rock that day 20 years ago camera crews would be camped outside your home for weeks leading up to the trial. They decided to leave you alone for now, in hopes you will tell what really happened in that hotel room when they call you as a witness in the trial. They say you are already on their preliminary witness list, will be on their final list and definitely will be called to testify in the trial.

You may be aware of this. But they know about Phil and Norma and claim they both have said they would testify truthfully if called to testify in the trial. They are unaware I have talked to both......or at least they didn't mention it.

I don't know yet whether Starr will subpoena either Norma or Phil, but am led to believe that his office has talked to at least one of them. Starr has been busy with other issues and, as you know, has not gotten around to any of the Jane Doe subpoenas. I'm told that he will, but that everything is taking longer than expected.

One thing of which I AM certain after many years of covering these kinds of stories is that your story will, at some point, come out in some form. It may be thru Starr or at the Jones trial. It may be because some other reporter gets wind of the story and decides to go with it, even without your participation. These things have a life of their own. And there are so many different media outlets these days that SOMEONE somewhere will print or air some version of it and then the frenzy will begin.

The worst thing that can happen is if the story starts to come out in pieces, or inaccurately. Then, you will have the worst of both worlds. Your name and allegations will be known to the world...but in a form that the White House has time to pick apart.

As a woman who has been thru a similar but less traumatic experience, I understand that having all this hanging over your head must re-open wounds...assuming they ever completely healed. It also must be difficult hearing some of the things being said about the President and know what you know. Given the kind of person you seem to be, some part of you at must at times be tempted to come forward and tell what happened. You know that these other women are not making this up.

From what I hear, Juanita Broaddrick is a person of integrity and strength, a person who runs the best nursing homes in the state and is sure that everything is done in the RIGHT way...(and a formidable tennis player to boot.....especially at doubles!)

Only you can decide what is best for you. As someone's whose job is to get to the truth of things, I ask you to consider whether you couldn't find a way to help me tell your story....in a dignified, sensitive way. It is a powerful story. And, given the current climate it would be impossible for the White House to retaliate against you or anyone who supported you....just for telling the truth. Norma and Phil are on the record and have said they will stand by you.

If you decide the story IS going to come out in some way, it is in your best interest that it be all at once, in full, and accurately. First, that minimizes the frenzy because there aren't a lot of details to keep digging up. (Which is what prolongs stories) Second, it is tougher for the White House to attack if the story comes out in full, accurately, and with supporting witnesses.

You may wonder why I won't give up on this. It's because I think this is a powerful and critically important story. Partly because you are not the kind of person who makes this up. And partly because I don't think anyone should be able to do what was done to you and get away with it.

I know that you worry that your life will never be the same if you finally come forward. But I don't think it would be as permanently changed as you and David fear. Remember, you DID NOT seek this attention. You have been pulled into this because of legal proceedings....and because of the act of someone else many years ago. What's more there are so many women out there by now...albeit it with different stories...that you are not alone. And I think the public would react to you with sympathy, empathy and respect for your courage.

Again, I appeal to your conscience. I know that to do what I am asking would take great courage. But I do believe the story

*will come out in some way. NBC NEWS has DATELINE NBC
as well as other broadcasts that would enable you to tell your
story in full. From the facts about what happened, from your
pact with Norma never to talk about it for fear you wouldn't be
believed or your nursing home would be retaliated against, to
your extreme reluctance to talk about it even now.*

*You could even make the point in the interview that you have
agreed to talk about this ONCE because you feel the nation has
a right to know, but that this would be your ONLY public
comment. (That would dissuade a lot of people from camping
out on your doorstep)*

*I am enclosing an article from the NY TIMES having to do with
Kathleen Willey, to show you that when a news organization
goes with a story like this, we also put OUR credibility on the
line. We would not air a story that we did not believe to be
true. Plus, unlike Willey, you would have two other people
(Norma and Phil) to back you up.*

*Please think about this. Kevin knows where to reach me at any
hour should you be willing to talk. We would be happy to fly
you and your family to Washington for any interview if you
want to avoid TV cameras coming to your home.*

Best Wishes,

*Lisa Myers
National Correspondent
NBC NEWS*

After I received this letter from Lisa, she and I began several
months of talking on the phone. I would agree to come
forward and then I would back out. David did not want me to
come forward. In late 1998 or early 1999, Lisa and her
producer flew to Fort Smith to meet with Kevin in hopes he
could persuade me. I told Kevin I wouldn't meet with her and
had decided not to do the interview. I knew he was going to
her hotel to meet with her and discuss my decision. I don't
know what changed my mind, but I wanted to meet Lisa in

person and that's exactly what I did. This was a big step for me. I showed up at the hotel and surprised both of them and myself, too. I sat down with Lisa, Kevin and Lisa's producer and began to discuss a possible interview. Before I left the hotel, I had decided it was the right thing to do. I was going to tell my story to the world.

Before I agreed to do the interview with Lisa, I had been having an ongoing email and phone discussion with a reporter from the Weekly Standard, Matt Labash. Our communications went on for months while I was also communicating with Lisa Myers. Matt wanted his magazine to do an exclusive with me, but I kept leaning toward Lisa and he knew I had developed a sincere friendship with her. Matt was an investigative reporter and very good at his job. He continually fired questions at me and unknowingly helped me remember details I would later relate to Lisa in the Dateline interview. He was very persistent and this helped me think long and hard about my statements, making sure my recollection was accurate. I still have copies of all of our emails. When I finally told Matt I was going to do the interview with Lisa, he was, of course, not happy with my decision. I never had a sense that he truly believed me, but after the Dateline interviewed aired, he contacted me. He said he watched the interview with his dad and his dad said to him "That woman is telling the truth." He agreed with his dad and I thanked him.

NBC DATELINE INTERVIEW, JANUARY 20, 1999

In the next few days, Lisa called and told me she and the camera crew would be at my home on the morning of January 20, 1999. This was really happening. I thought to myself, "Am I really going to do this?" It was all moving so fast, my head was spinning. I knew it was the right thing to do, but I was so frightened at the very thought of bearing my soul on national television. I would be explaining the most horrific event of my life to millions of people. Also, Lisa told me it would be necessary to tell about my extramarital affair with David. It was overwhelming.

The day came and the camera crew show up and transformed my living room into a television studio. I was so nervous. While I was in my bathroom getting ready I started crying. I remember thinking, "I can't do this and I have to tell Lisa." I am going to have to tell them to take all of those cameras and lights out of my house and just go away. David was very supportive and calmed me down. He told me he knew I could do this interview and he was proud of me. I hugged him and then redid my make up for the interview.

It began. I told about my volunteering in Bill Clinton's campaign for Governor and what led up to my meeting in private with him. Then it came time to talk about the rape. I began to cry and ask for the cameras to stop so I could compose myself. It seems like the interview lasted for hours, but the Dateline segment was edited down to about 30 minutes. There is one important thing I need to bring up here. When Lisa asked if I had ever been threatened or intimidated by anyone, I began to talk about my meeting with Hillary 20 years earlier and how she had threatened me. It was at this time, the producer called out to stop and came into the room and said, "We can't go there. We cannot discuss Hillary." Lisa and I looked at each other in surprise. Lisa asked the question a second time. I replied "No." I had no idea why I couldn't talk about Hillary but was told I couldn't. It wasn't right for the producer not to allow a very important part of my story. When Lisa asked the question for the second time, I should have said, yes. I was threatened but NBC will not allow me to talk about it. I said no because I had only been threatened by Hillary.

In the 2016 Presidential race, I would bring up the decades old threatening encounter with Hillary. Her supporters would ask why I was just now bringing this to light. I have talked about it for years and even gave an interview with Sean Hannity a very few years after Dateline about my encounter with Hillary. I wasn't just now bringing this up because she was running for President. I had been on record talking about it many years before. I even sent an open letter to Hillary that was published in many online news such as Free Republic.com, truthfeed.com, americanconservative.com, thenewamerican.com and many more.

AN OPEN LETTER TO HILLARY CLINTON,
BY JUANITA BROADDRICK

'DO YOU REMEMBER?'
SUNDAY OCT 15, 2000

As I watched Rick Lazio's interview on Fox News this morning, I felt compelled to write this open letter to you, Mrs. Clinton. Brit Hume asked Mr. Lazio's views regarding you as a person and how he perceived you as a candidate. Rick Lazio did not answer the question, but I know that I can. You know it, too. I have no doubt that you are the same conniving, self-serving person you were twenty-two years ago when I had the misfortune to meet you in person. When I see you on television, campaigning for the New York senate race, I can see the same hypocrisy in your face that you displayed to me one evening in 1978. You have not changed.

I remember it as though it was yesterday. I only wish that it were yesterday and maybe there would still be time to do something about what your husband, Bill Clinton, did to me. There was a political rally for Mr. Clinton's bid for governor of

Arkansas. I had obligated myself to be at this rally prior to my being assaulted by your husband in April, 1978. I had made up my mind to make an appearance and then leave as soon as the two of you arrived. This was a big mistake, but I was still in a state of shock and denial. You had questioned the gentleman who drove you and Mr. Clinton from the airport. You asked him about me and if I would be at the gathering. Do you remember? You told the driver, "Bill has talked so much about Juanita," and that you were so anxious to meet me. Well, you wasted no time. As soon as you entered the room, you came directly to me and grabbed my hand. Do you remember how you thanked me, saying "we want to thank you for everything that you do for Bill?" At that point, I was pretty shaken and started to walk off. Remember how you kept a tight grip on my hand and drew closer to me? You repeated your statement, but this time with a coldness and look that I have seen many times on television in the last eight years. You said, "Everything you do for Bill." You then released your grip and I said nothing and left the gathering.

What did you mean, Hillary? Were you referring to my keeping quiet about the assault I had suffered at the hands of your husband only two weeks before? Were you warning me to continue to keep quiet? We both know the answer to that question. Yes, I can answer Brit Hume's question. You are the same Hillary that you were twenty years ago. You are cold, calculating and self-serving. You cannot tolerate the thought that you will soon be without the power you have wielded for the last eight years. Your effort to stay in power will be at the expense of the state of New York. I only hope the voters of New York will wake up in time and realize that Hillary Clinton is not an honorable or an honest person.

I will end by asking if you believe the statements I made on NBC Dateline when Lisa Myers asked if I had been assaulted and raped by your husband. Or perhaps, you are like Vice-President Gore and did not see the interview.

Juanita Broaddrick
Arkansas

Lisa Myers and her camera crew left the next day, taking with them my story, laid out in living color, tears and all. She told me that the investigation process was over and it would air on January 29, 1999, while the impeachment trial was still ongoing. I waited, but there was no announcement of the airing. Lisa would phone and say that NBC had a few more details to investigate and it should be scheduled soon. The word had gotten out that NBC vehicles had been at my home and more news outlets began to call my home. Other news outlets were reporting that the interview had taken place. I ignored their calls and messages. I waited, but there was no indication when the interview would air.

About two to three weeks after the interview, David and I were snow skiing in Breckenridge with our boys. I was depressed about the interview not being aired as planned on January 29, but trying to enjoy this family time. Lisa called and told me that a group of NBC news people had view the tape of my interview, including Tim Russert and other executives. I'll never forget her statement to me. She said, "I have good news and I have bad news." My heart sank. Here it comes. They are not going to air it. She continued, "The good news is you're credible...... (pause)...the bad news is you're very credible." What a blow. I did not immediately understand the impact of that statement. I was told by another NBC person that Andrew Lack, President of NBC news, wanted further investigation into my story before it could be aired. She also commented that Andrew Lack and Bill Clinton were friends and often golfed together. How convenient for Bill Clinton.

There it was. NBC was holding the story and as many would say later, until after Clinton's impeachment trial was over. I was so hurt and took my frustrations out on the one person I should have trusted, Lisa Myers. She was standing firmly by our interview, but I was angry and told her not to call me again. I felt betrayed and I took it out on her. This was so wrong. She had supported me in every way. I learned later how she fought for me and this important interview. At the same time, someone invented a slogan relating to the interview not being aired. It was, "Free Lisa Myers." I remember Brit Hume and others on FOX News Special Report bravely wearing a "Free

Lisa Myers" button on air. I was thankful for his courage and support and admire him to this day. Lisa and I have remained friends all these years. She is my hero.

On May 25, 2016, Hume talked about this incident to RealClearPolitics.com:

BRIT HUME: Back at the time when all of these allegations against President Clinton were surfacing, the woman, Juanita Broaddrick, who appears in this Trump ad, accused the president of rape. Of raping her in a hotel room in Little Rock. Her charges were specific. She was who she said she was. There's no doubt about that. A lot of us found the allegations credible, at least credible to the point where they bore serious investigation. I always believed, based on the rest of his conduct, that the allegations were likely true.

NBC News' Lisa Myers did an interview with Juanita Broaddrick, in which she explained the whole thing. It was pretty powerful stuff. NBC sat on it for a long time. To the point where, back when I was anchor of Special Report, we went on the air with "Free Lisa Myers" buttons. I found it, kept it all these years.

DOROTHY RABINOWITZ AND THE WALL STREET JOURNAL

It was during this time that I received a phone call from Dorothy Rabinowitz of the Wall Street Journal wanting to interview me. I was fed up with reporters and wanted nothing to do with her. I was polite and told her no. She said she was flying in to Little Rock in the next few days and would contact me then, hoping I would change my mind. I told her to please not come and that I would not change my mind. She had a kind voice and I liked her, but as I said, I had had enough of being used by the media.

A few days later, she calls me and says she is in Little Rock and going to drive to Van Buren in the hope I would reconsider. Again I told her, there was no need to come because I had not changed my mind. I thought that was the end of that. A few hours later, I received a phone call from a young lady who said she was Dorothy's driver and they were at my gate!! Good Lord, this woman wouldn't take no for an answer. I again told her no, I would not be interviewed. There was a pause.....and the driver said, "Can Ms. Rabinowitz just come up to use your bathroom?" I was dumbfounded. She had passed many bathroom facilities along the way. I don't know what made me say it, but I replied that she could.

Here they came up the drive. The driver and Dorothy got out and came to my front door where I was waiting. She introduced herself and I ask them in and showed her the way to the bathroom. I remember thinking how dignified and elegant she was in her appearance. I had researched her after her first calls to me and found she was known for her excellence in newspaper journalism. She wasn't here to play cat and mouse with me. She was here for an interview. I was still upset with NBC's delays and thought to myself, "Why not?" And so, the interview began. We sat in the living room and talked. Then, my story began to roll out of me like an avalanche. We talked for a couple of hours and continued to talk on the phone when she returned home.

The Wall Street Journal article, "Juanita Broaddrick Meets The Press," came out on February 19, 1999. I was very happy with the article and felt vindicated by it. Dorothy Rabinowitz had a way with words. They flowed delicately, but yet harshly in her description of Bill Clinton's scandalous as well as criminal behavior with women. What's more important, she, like Lisa Myers, believed me. They knew I was telling the truth. I respect both of them to this day for having the courage to stand with me.

Dorothy Rabinowitz was awarded the 2001 Pulitzer Prize For Commentary for a series of articles covering social and cultural trends. She had been nominated in previous years, but this was her first Pulitzer. She also sat on a panel on CNN's Larry King Live show when my son was interviewed on March 8, 1999, approximately two weeks after my NBC Dateline interview. Others on the panel discussing my son's interview were David Gergen, Dee Dee Myers and Jeff Greenfield. This interview was never shown again and unavailable online. It is now available to view at Juanitabroaddrick.com. It is a remarkable and revealing interview.

NBC AIRS DATELINE INTERVIEW OPPOSITE THE GRAMMYS

Was it the publishing of the Wall Street Journal article or public outrage that forced NBC to air my long overdue Dateline interview? Or, was it because the impeachment hearing of Bill Clinton was now over? I will probably never know the answer to these questions. It was scheduled to run opposite of the Grammy Awards and I really didn't care. It had missed the window of opportunity with the impeachment hearing and it no longer mattered to me when it was aired. True justification had come with the WSJ article by Dorothy Rabinowitz.

My family gathered to watch the interview and I was very apprehensive, wondering what the final product would be like after the editing of over 5 hours of taping. It started. I watched up until I tearfully began to talk about the rape. I had to leave the room and never watched the entire interview, until 2016, when I became involved in my own campaign to stop Hillary Clinton's run for president. It had been too painful to watch decades ago and still was. The Dateline interview had come to the forefront in the presidential campaign because of my tweet that went viral on 1-6-2016. I had responded to a tweet Hillary Clinton had made a few weeks earlier. I will discuss this later in my story.

It was over. I had done the one thing I had dreaded to do for over 20 years. Media polls were taken on whether people believed me or not and thankfully, the percentages were predominately in my favor. The negative comments were very few and far between and I tried to not let them upset me. I had done the best I knew how and it was over, done, finished and laid out for all the world to see. Of all of the NBC Dateline episodes rebroadcast over the years, this was never one of them. It aired once and never again.

Feminist organizations and Women's Rights Leaders ignored me and never supported me. This was sad and so hurtful. They were on good terms with President Clinton and did not want to be at odds with the White House. They were working closely with the administration and had Bill Clinton's ear as well as his support. They threw me under the bus to continue along this path of their legislative agenda. During the Monica Lewinsky scandal, Betty Friedman said, "Clinton's enemies are attempting to bring him down over some dalliance with an intern. Whether it's true or not, I simply don't care," and would not answer questions about my allegations. These women's groups decided right away that Bill Clinton's support outweighed the criminal sordidness of his personal life.

During the Monica Lewinsky headlines, Gloria Steinem made the statement, "If Bill Clinton had raped women or beaten Hillary, and real sins would not be forgiven no matter the value of public behavior." Patricia Ireland, NOW president said, "We need to stop wasting our time on unproven charges." After Kathleen Willey came forward in 1998, Anita Ferguson stated, "There's no question, these accusations are disturbing." When I came forward in 1999, not one person from any of these feminist groups ever contacted me. Not one.

SECOND MARRIAGE COLLAPSES

After the Dateline interview, my life as a mother, wife and business woman began to return to as normal as could be expected under the circumstances. I would continue to have phone calls and emails from various media outlets. It was intense for many months and then it began slowly disappearing. There was a noticeable strain between David and me. We were not getting along and it was mostly my fault. We probably should have sought counseling, but we did not. We separated in 2002 and the divorced many months later.

It was not an amicable divorce. We had so many financial connections to sort out. It was finally agreed that I would keep our home, my nursing home and he would buy my shares in the children's facility. I believe David truly loved me, but I had grown into a person who was battling emotional issues from the rape as well as the interview. I was not an easy person to live with. He also had problems that I will not go into. He deserves that from me. He was a good father to his boys and a good step-father to Kevin.

A few months after my second divorce was final, I received a call from Sean Hannity requesting an interview. I watched his show regularly back then and I had a lot of respect for Sean. I agreed to do it. The Fox crew and Sean arrived at my home on June 11, 2003. We talked about my rape by Bill Clinton and my encounter with Hillary Clinton approximately 2-3 weeks later. I don't think Sean was prepared to hear my description of the horrific events of April 25, 1978, even though he had seen my interview with Lisa Myers and was familiar with what had occurred. At one point in the interview he became so moved that I actually saw tears in his eyes. This was the first time I realized who Sean Hannity really was. He truly cared about what had happened to me and other victims and he hasn't changed today. I consider him a great American and a friend.

After my interview with Sean, I settled back into the life as a single woman with a business to run. I would travel with family and friends and enjoyed a good life. My son was a successful attorney and the proud new father of a beautiful baby boy. I was putting the past behind me and looking to the future. I was very content for the next few years. By 2008, I was growing tired of the day to day effort that it took to maintain a well-run facility. It had been 34 years and it was time to think about retiring. I decided to do just that and began the search for the right person(s) to take over. The new owners are good people and I feel I have left my business in good hands. All those years of struggling to make Brownwood Manor a reality were now gone but never forgotten. I had worked diligently for over 47 years at everything I had attempted, from nurses training to running my own businesses. I could not sell the name, Brownwood Manor, with the business because it was too personal to me. It is now called Van Buren Health and Rehabilitation. I will see people around town and they still refer to it as Brownwood even though it has been almost ten years since it changed names. It will always be Brownwood to me, too.

SIDETRACKED INTO AFRICA

In 2006, two years before I retired, I was at my computer and received a yahoo alert that someone in Africa was messaging me. I thought, what the heck, and accepted the message. It was from a man, Constant Jallah, who was residing in the Buduburham refugee camp in Accra, Ghana. He began to tell me of his family's struggles as a Liberian refugee. He never asked me for money. He just wanted to have someone to talk to. We began to email back and forth for many weeks. Then one day I asked him how I could help and where I could send money to him and his family. This began many years of my financial assistance, by way of Western Union, to the family.

Constant's family included two brothers, one sister, a girlfriend who was the mother of his four year old son, and two unrelated young brothers they had taken in. He related how they were citizens in Liberia during Charles Taylor's wars against humanity, Taylor being one of the most prominent war lords in African history. There was a movie made about this inhumane treatment called "Blood Diamonds." Constant told me how his mother and father were murdered in front of him and his siblings. They were forced to remove their parents clothing and bury them. They were then placed in bondage and used as labor for the soldiers of Taylor. He told me they were awaiting their execution when they were rescued. They became members of the Liberian Boat People. After almost 2 months at sea these refugees were finally accepted by Sierra Leone and Ghana. Constant and his family were processed in Ghana and transferred to Buduburham Refugee Camp in Accra, Ghana.

Constant was in an internet cafe in the Buduburham camp when he messaged me. I feel like this might be what you call divine intervention. Who really know? There I was at my computer one day at the very moment he was reaching out. He needed help and I was one who could give it. There was no running water and the conditions were deplorable in the quarters he and his family were living at Buduburham. His son, Tolos, had already suffered malaria as well as diseases from contaminated water. I sent him enough money to move his family to an apartment in the town of Accra. The new home suited them very nicely and they were happy for the time being.

I continued to send money for food and rent for the next several months. I even went to Walmart and purchased clothing and shipped it to them, but the shipping cost were as much as the clothing. I decided that was not the best thing to do. This was beginning to add up. I decided it was time to go to Ghana and see exactly where the money was going. I felt this family was truly who they said they were but I needed to see for myself.

I had become good friends with Julia Malone, a newspaper reporter for Cox Newspapers in Washington, DC, during the media blitz after the Dateline interview. She had been very supportive of my story. I called Julia one day and asked if she would like to go with me to Africa to meet the Jallah family. She immediately said "absolutely not." Then about a week later she phoned to say, yes, she would go, but she was going to plan our trip. Thank goodness, because I was at a loss where to start first and Julia was a seasoned traveler.

We left from DC on our long trek to South Africa. Julia had gone to great lengths to plan a wonderful three week excursion around Johannesburg, Cape Town, Zimbabwe, Botswana, and others and then on to Ghana for the last week. We went on the most fabulous safari trips. Then it was on to Accra to meet the adopted family.

When we arrived at the Accra airport, we went through a long tunnel and as we emerged from the other side, there they stood shouting Mama and holding up a sign with a picture of me. Julia and I looked at each other in total amazement.

We left the airport in several taxi's to go to their home. When we arrived, I was happy to see the iron gate at the entrance. The Ghana people did not take kindly to the Liberian refugees who had been woven into their economy by their government. Liberian refugees were threatened on a daily basis. The apartment consisted of several rooms not attached to each other for bedrooms and one large room with dilapidated old furniture and a television. There was a makeshift dining table and chairs, but no kitchen, per say. They cooked outside over an open fire. There were no beds, just bedding and sometimes mattresses on the floor, but they were happy. I had brought more clothing for them in my suitcases and they were excitedly going through all I had brought.

We then left for our hotel and made arrangements to have them meet us at our hotel for dinner the next evening. We had reserved a large table for all of us. At first there was a problem with the restaurant not wanting to serve them, and this broke my heart. I spoke with the person in charge and told them that these were my "adopted" children and this seemed to ease the situation. The Jallah family never seemed to relax throughout the dinner, though. I guess the situation between the Liberian refugees and Ghana people was worse than I had realized.

Julia and I spent the next few days touring around Ghana and visiting with my new family. It was a joyful time for all of us. When it was time to leave, there were tears and hugs and promises to continue my financial assistance to them. They were everything I hoped they would be and Julia agreed and she, also, began to help them financially.

After several months, Constant express his desire to return to Liberia. Liberia had a new president, Ellen Johnson Sirleaf. She had been educated in the US and had a master's degree from Harvard University School of Government and was making great efforts in turning the war torn country around. Constant wanted to take his family home. We made arrangements to buy a plot of land to build a home. I purchased many airfare tickets for Constant to go to Liberia to buy the land and for subsequent trips to hand make building blocks. Blocks could not be purchased and had to be made at the building site. He had an uncle and cousins in Monrovia who would help make the blocks and were overjoyed to have the income. They built a makeshift building for the uncle to stay in and to store the blocks. Crime was still rampant and the building materials had to be guarded. The work was very hard and he would stay a month and then return to Accra to rest for a few weeks.

This process went on for over a year. Finally it was time to build the long awaited home. Construction was completed in about 4 months except for windows and doors. These had to be steel due to the criminal situation in Monrovia. If you didn't have steel, your home would definitely be broken into. It took another six months for these to be manufactured. Finally, they were ready to make the final flight to their homeland. It was exciting. I sent enough money for airfare for the entire family group. Sadly, the two adopted brothers, Constant's sister and one brother decided not to go and spent their airfare money on other things. They are still in Accra, Ghana, but I do not correspond with them.

Constant, his girlfriend, Viola, his son, Tolos, and his brother, Chris, returned to Liberia and their new home in 2010. They are self-sufficient now selling used jeans from a cart in the marketplace. They purchase lots of used jeans for $150 and are able to sell them for $300. Constant and Viola were married a year after they arrived in Monrovia and now have added twins to their family. Their names are Jonathan and Juanita. I am so proud they named their daughter after me. They all still live together in the home. I am truly fortunate to have been able to help this wonderful family.

MY MOTHER COMES BACK INTO MY LIFE

The day I bought mom's half of Brownwood Manor, I told her if she ever needed me to call, but that I would not contact her. In 2009, I received a call from one of my mother's friend, Hazel Moore. She told me that my mom was not doing well and that my mom wanted me to call her. We hadn't spoken in four years. I called and went to see her that very day. My niece had been caring for mom and was her power of attorney. Mom had a very nice home but I immediately saw that the conditions were not good. The home was in dire need of housekeeping and repair from a recent storm. My niece and I did not get along but my mom needed help and she wanted that help from me. It reminded me of when dad died. It felt good to be needed by her. I hired someone to clean her home and would visit her daily. We would go out to eat and to the local casino. She loved to play the slot machines.

Eventually, she had to be moved to an assisted living facility and her home was sold. I became mom's power of attorney. She was not getting along with my niece, but this was mom's usual pattern, switching alliances from one family member to another. When she came to the point of needing more assistance, I hired a private duty nurse to be with her at night when the facility had so few employees to meet her needs.

Sometimes, when we were together, I would see what I thought was remorse in her eyes as she looked at me. It took me back to those times when I was a child, watching her as she worked at the cleaning business. It was like she wanted to say "I'm sorry," but didn't know how. I went to the facility every day. One day she asked to move in with me. I knew there was no way this would work. I had my own life to live and her dementia caused her to yell at all intervals of the day and night.

Soon, she required more care than assisted living could provide even during the day hours. She had numerous medical issues along with the dementia and required continuous supervision and care. She always had a fear of being placed in a nursing home and I promised her I would never do that. I made arrangements for the construction of a mobile home with handicapped accommodations and had it placed next to my home. I hired nurses to care for her around the clock. She seemed to love her new little home. I would go over every morning to have coffee with her. Her mind wandered but she always knew who I was.

I bought a motorhome and took mom and her nurses on many trips. We equipped the motorhome with everything we needed for her care. It had two bedrooms and two bathrooms. The couch made a bed for one of the nurses while the other would watch mom during the night. I would wear earplugs at night to diminish the sounds of her dementia because I was the driver and needed my sleep. She would sit in the passenger seat next to me. When she would start to yell, I would calmly say, "Mom, please try not to yell." She would look over at me with a bewildered expression and say, "I'm not yelling." I finally accustomed myself to it because it was something she couldn't control.

We took her to the beach in Florida, to the gambling casinos in Biloxi, Mississippi and short excursions to Tulsa and Fayetteville for a day out. In Destin, Florida, we found a mobile home park that was right on the beach and stayed there for 3 days. We sat up a small pavilion tent in front of the motorhome and would take her out there. She would sit quietly in her lounge chair during these times, looking out at the ocean and seemed to be in a trance. I would watch her and wonder what she was thinking, but I will never know. If I spoke to her, it would only bring on the yelling, so I kept quiet and enjoyed the view along with her.

It was an adventure for all of us, but she became too difficult to manage while traveling. Eventually, we could no longer take her out on even short trips. She died after only nine month in her new little home. She had always expressed her wishes to be cremated when she was still alert and coherent. I asked what she wanted me to do with her ashes. She said whatever I wanted to do with them. She didn't care. After her memorial service, my sister and I went to the cemetery and spread her ashes on my dad's grave. We said our prayers and left. I closed another chapter of my life. Both of my parents were gone and I lost my sister in 2015 to heart disease. I miss them.

A 73-YEAR-OLD WOMAN LEARNS TWITTER

Where do I begin to tell about my involvement in the 2016 campaign for President of the United States? I had no particular interest in becoming involved and did not ever want to talk about my rape by Bill Clinton, again. Then in September, 2015, Hillary Clinton made a speech containing this message: "I want to send a message to every survivor of sexual assault: Don't let anyone silence your voice. You have the right to be heard. You have the right to be believed and we're with you." This section of her speech went to her website and the response could not have been what she was hoping for, says thedailycaller.com. This was undoubtedly the stupidest comment that Hillary Clinton could ever have made. It was as though she was oblivious to her husband's past or she was flaunting it and daring anyone to question her. The public outrage went viral on twitter and I went ballistic.

I had opened a Twitter account a couple of years earlier, but really didn't understand how to use it. I knew I couldn't stay quiet any longer and I had to reply to this ridiculous statement. I didn't know quite what to do. I worked on a statement to reply to Hillary. The tweet wouldn't go through. I kept trying with no results. I finally called my 12-year-old grandson and asked him for help. I did not tell him what I was tweeting, because he was unaware of what had happened to me in 1978. I followed his instructions and finally had an acceptable number of letters in my tweet. I was pleased with my statement and felt it was a good response. Then I pressed the tweet symbol.

January 6, 2016, Juanita Broaddrick@atensnut tweeted the following:
I was 35 years old when Bill Clinton, Ark. Attorney General raped me and Hillary tried to silence me. I am now 73.....it never goes away.

ALL HELL BROKE LOOSE! Within 20 minutes, my phone was ringing off the wall with reporters calling. My tweet had gone viral. I had only wanted to make a comment and let Hillary know I was having none her bullshit! (I am sure there is a more appropriate word, but that is what comes to mind) My son, Kevin, called within an hour or two asking me if I had really thought this through and what the consequences might be. I was unable to answer him intelligently and was beginning to think I had made a huge mistake. The phone continued to ring and I was letting it go to my answering unit. Reporter after reporter leaving request for comments. What on earth had I done? I had absolutely no idea of the power of Twitter but it was done and I had to face the music. Now, I needed to explain my tweet to those who had never heard my name or the revelations I made about Bill Clinton decades ago. I also wanted to speak to those who were aware and ready to lend their support once again.

I happen to answer the phone when Andrea Mitchell called later that afternoon. She wanted me to go to a local NBC affiliate to be interview about my statement on Twitter. I told her I would not do that and she opted for a phone interview that would be played on the evening news. She began recording what I soon realized to be a hostile interview. She kept trying to put words in my mouth about what I interpreted as threats from Hillary on that evening in 1978. She kept asking, "How do you know that is what she meant?" I did not back down from my statement and told her she would have to have been standing in my shoes at that moment in time. I knew I had been threatened by Hillary and would have nothing to do with Andrea Mitchell's interpretation of a conversation she knew nothing about. We finished the interview. A few moments later, Andrea called back and said they weren't going to run the interview because there was nothing new to report.

I had no idea of the power of Twitter. I was a senior citizen with a limited knowledge of social media. I was telling my story once again but this time it was immediate and to the world. I had about 6 followers prior to 1-6-2016 and within a day it grew to over a 1000. So much happened in such a short time. The negative tweets were very few and I soon realized these people were just cowards hiding behind their keyboards. When I was attacked and threatened on Twitter, my followers would shut them down almost immediately. This was surprising as well as heartwarming. After I made my statement on Twitter, I learned Hillary's statement, "You should be believed," was removed from her website. Hillary's campaign knew she had erred in a big way. I now have nearly 70,000 followers.

My son, Kevin, was also on Twitter and he cautioned me many times to be careful about what I tweeted. He was very concerned about my well-being and the well-being of my family. We would have disagreements, but he finally realized I could not remain silent any longer. For decades I had been told that my accusations were old news and nobody wanted to hear from me. Twitter gave me a voice and I was going to use it. It made me wonder what the impeachment hearing would have been like had Twitter existed back then. I sound like a Twitter commercial, but you must realize what it did for me. It not only gave me a renewed strength and courage, it also gave me hope that the Clintons might actually be held accountable for their crimes.

I was not a Trump supporter in the beginning. I thought his comments were unorganized and careless. It took me a few months to realize that he was neither careless nor unorganized. He was crafty and cunning and I finally decided he was the one I wanted to support. He was exactly what the American people had been hoping for after the failed presidency of Barack Obama. Donald J. Trump could possibly be our next president and I wanted to help in every possible way. I climbed on the Trump bandwagon.

Once Twitter propelled me into the news, the liberal media began to spin their own version of what had happened so many decades ago. I had denied the rape in depositions for the Paula Jones case; therefore, they concluded I was not telling the truth in my statement to the independent counsel, in which I gave details about my rape by Bill Clinton. I was able to instantly refute inaccurate information from biased and/or liberal news media and pundits. I can understand why Mr. Trump used Twitter throughout his campaign and continues to use it after his election. It is instant and goes directly to the people and not through the media.

I watched as Sean Hannity interviewed Donald Trump on the evening of on May 18, 2016. Hannity began to ask questions about a recent unflattering New York Times' story involving Mr. Trump's relationships with women. Hannity asks Trump, "I looked at the New York Times. Are they going to interview Juanita Broaddrick? Are they going to interview Paula Jones? Are they going to interview Kathleen Willey? In one case, it's about exposure. In another case it's about groping and fondling against a woman's will." Then Trump finishes Hannity's sentence and said, "And rape."

There "IT" was in all of its horrifying glory. The word I had been so hesitant to say most of my life.....RAPE. The very same word that was coaxed out of me by Lisa Myers on NBC Dateline but this time it had come out of Donald Trump's mouth. You could have knocked me over with a feather. It not only shocked me, it also gave me corroboration. I had grown accustomed to saying sexual assault for so many years, because the word rape was too horrendous and descriptive. For the first time in many years, I felt empowered to say the word rape to describe the most horrific event in my life. What Bill Clinton did to me was rape. The media was in a state of shock. How would they spin this? How could they make Trump the bad man instead of true predator, Bill Clinton?

The next morning after the Fox News Trump interview, the NBC Today show featured a segment by Andrea Mitchell discussing Trump's comments on Sean Hannity and specifically the word rape in describing Bill Clinton's past. Mitchell proceeded to refer to my allegations as "discredited" and long denied by Clinton. I was completely dumbfounded that she had the audacity to make this false statement on national television. My allegations against Bill Clinton have never been discredited. This was a personal assault on me by NBC, but particularly by Andrea Mitchell, who was a Hillary Clinton supporter. Then, I was remembered our phone conversation on January 6, 2016. Now, almost 5 months later she was saying to me, "I'll have the last word." No so quick, Andrea!

My attorney and son, Kevin Hickey, sent a letter to Andy Lack, President of NBC News. It demanded a retraction of the word "discredited" from any future airing of the Mitchell statement and removal of the word from the NBC Website or a lawsuit would certainly follow. In a matter of days, NBC complied. It was a win for us although we felt an on-air retraction on the Today Show was more appropriate. I was relieved and so proud of my son, Kevin. I have often wondered if Andrea Mitchell had coordinated her efforts with the Clinton campaign in her spiteful attempt to "discredit" me.

On October 6, 2016, The Washington Post released a taped conversation and video from a 2005 conversation between Donald Trump and Billy Bush. It caused an immediate uproar from the liberal media, calling for Trump's resignation from the presidential race. The video/audio tape was very upsetting to me as I listened to the lewd remarks about women by Mr. Trump. How could I possibly continue to support Donald Trump? The next day, as I watched Mr. Trump's 3 minute video response about the unfortunate recording, I saw a man very remorseful and apologetic about the careless comments he had made over a decade ago. He referred to it as "locker room talk." I believed him and along with millions of others and accepted his apology. These words were disgusting and regrettable but they could never compare to the rape I suffered at the hands of Bill Clinton. It was later learned that the Washington Post was given the tape by NBC, according to unidentified TMZ sources.

TWITTER: October 8, 2016, Juanita Broaddrick@atensnut (retweeted by Donald Trump)
How many times must it be said? Actions speak louder than words. DT said bad things! HRC threatened me after BC raped me.

THE PRESIDENTIAL DEBATE

During 2015-16, Kathleen Willey, Paula Jones McFadden and I had become acquainted with Aaron Klein, an investigative reporter at Breitbart. He had interviewed each of us for Breitbart articles and we had been guests on his radio show. He contacted us in September wanting to bring the three of us to DC for a special   sit down interview and videotaping. The plans were to interview each of us individually and then all three of us together. We all agreed and flew to DC on October 6, 2016 for the interview. It was filmed the next day at the historic Watergate Hotel. Kathleen and I had met over ten years ago and had spoken many times over the phone. I had never met Paula Jones in person until the day before the interview.

I was comfortable during the group interview but as it grew closer to my individual interview, I told Aaron that I didn't know if I could go through the details of the rape without becoming emotional. He said he understood and we could stop anytime I needed a break. You would think after all these years it would get easier to talk about it.........it does not! I was almost shaking when the time came for my interview. I walked in and sat down across from Aaron and it began. When it came time to talk about the rape, I tried not to cry, but just like in the dateline interview in 1999, as I began to tell the agonizing details, all the memories came flooding back along with the tears.

When the interview was over, I was completely drained. As I walked from the set, Kathleen Willey came over to me immediately and I broke down again. She put her arms around me and I started crying again. I will never forget what she said to me....."It's not your fault. It's not your fault. It's not your fault. You didn't do anything wrong. You didn't do anything wrong. Okay. Okay?" I will always be grateful for the compassion she showed to me that day. The Clintons had put this gentle woman through Hell and here she was expressing such kindness to me. She is a true hero.

We were through with filming and it was time to head back to Arkansas. I was on an airplane on the runway headed back to Arkansas. I had forgotten to turn off my cellphone and it was ringing. It was from the Trump campaign, inviting me to the second Presidential debate in St. Louis, Mo. I was told that Kathleen and Paula were also being invited. I was completely caught off guard. I told them I would have to think about it and I would call them back during my layover in Dallas. It was now 5 p.m. and I wouldn't get home until after midnight. I turned off my phone and began to think about the invitation. What precipitated this? Was the Trump campaign just using us?

I made the decision to go. I didn't care what had brought about the invitation. Bill Clinton's victims had been told for decades to go back into the woodwork and that our stories were not newsworthy. It was time to disagree with that notion and visibly support Donald Trump by our appearance. The media perception was, "This was not about Bill Clinton....Hillary was the candidate." Wrong....this had everything to do with a candidate running for the president of the United States who had threatened and intimidated her husband's victims.

During my layover in Dallas, I also phoned my son, Kevin, and told him about the invitation to the debate. He was still reeling from the Trump and Bush recording and asked me not to go. I knew he was disappointed that I could still support Trump after all the disgusting remarks he had made. I tried to explain and told him to look at the bigger picture, but it fell on deaf ears and I certainly didn't blame him. We agreed to disagree. He said, "Mom, just be careful. There are a lot of crazy Clinton supporters out there." I told him we had been assured of security if any situations arose.

I got home around 1 a.m. on October 9, 2016, repacked and was back on a plane to St. Louis at 7 a.m. The woman at the ticket counter smiled as she looked at my name and destination and said, "I bet I know where you are going." I guess the word got around because several other airport employees came over to me and expressed their support as I waited in line at the security check. Although I did not know any of these people, their comments were encouraging and very much appreciated.

The Trump campaign had instructed me to be as low profile as possible and that our appearance at the debate was being kept from the media. I was told my driver at the St. Louis airport would be holding a sign that said "Jane Morgan." This was amusing to me. I felt like a participant in some kind of covert operation and I guess, in fact, I was. I arrived in St. Louis before noon and began to look for my driver. Then I saw the sign bearing my new name. I went up to the gentleman and said, "Hi, I'm Jane Morgan." He responded, "Sure you are." We laughed and were on our way.

We meandered through traffic to the outskirts of St. Louis until we reached the hotel. It consisted of several buildings like apartments. Reporters covering the second debate were staying at this same hotel. When we pulled into a parking space, I was asked to stay in the car until it could be determined there were no reporters outside anywhere. After about 5 minutes, I was quickly ushered to a room where I was greeted by two young Trump campaign workers, Jared and Laura. They told me that Paula and Kathleen had not arrived in St. Louis, yet. Jared said it was important that I not leave the room and that they would be happy to get anything I needed. The refrigerator was loaded with all kinds of food and drinks. I was very tired from all the traveling and very little sleep and just wanted to lie down.

It was a little awkward, because they continued to stay in the room with me. Then, I learned it was actually Jared's room and mine was not ready yet. I laid down and rested, but couldn't sleep. Jared and Laura were constantly on their phones with the Trump organization. They kept asking questions to the people on the other end about times and tickets. Every now and then they would ask if I needed anything. It amused me and I thought, "Here are two very intelligent young people with important jobs on the Trump team and now have the added responsibility of keeping a 73-year-old woman hidden and happy." They succeeded.

About 4:30 p.m., I was told we would be leaving in about an hour to go to Mr. Trump's hotel to meet him prior to the debate. I still hadn't seen Kathleen but was told she was now in St. Louis and would be going with us to Trump's hotel. Paula had left D.C. and was on her way to St. Louis. It came time to leave the room and we went through the same procedure as when I arrived. I was to wait until the coast was clear and then proceed quickly to the car. I went to the car first and then Kathleen followed. When we arrived at the hotel, men were positioned at different areas outside Mr. Trump's hotel, directing us to the basement parking area. Kathleen and I were taken by way of a service elevator up to the top floor. We were taken to a large bright meeting room of sorts with a table full of more refreshments. I only wanted water. I was too nervous to eat anything.

As we entered the room, the first person I saw was Candice Jackson. Candice and I had met many years ago when she had written a book titled, "Their Lives," referring to Bill Clinton's victims. We had become friends and she had even been to my home in 2016 doing a follow-up article to her book. Candice and I had talked a couple of days before and keeping our agreement with the Trump people, had not told each other we were going to be the debate. We looked at each other and burst out laughing. I walked over and hugged her. She then introduced me to Kathy Shelton. Candice was a spokesperson for Kathy. It was a joy to meet Kathy and speak with her. Her story is heartbreaking.

In a few minutes, we were told to go into an adjoining room to meet Mr. Trump. As we entered the smaller room I saw a long table with five chairs. Shortly, Mr. Trump entered the room and came to each one of us expressing his sympathy for what we had been through and his appreciation for our being there. It was nice to meet him in person. I was surprised how soft spoken he was. Paula was still not there and I was beginning to wonder if she was going to make it. There was a problem with her flight scheduling from DC. We were told where to sit at the long table and that the middle seat was for Mr. Trump. We all sat down and I wondered what we were doing sitting at a table. Paula finally arrived and joined us at the table. Then I heard someone say "Let them in." Before I knew it, the door opened and in came reporters and cameras. Wow.....what was happening? The look on the reporters faces could not have been anymore baffling than the four women staring back at them.

Mr. Trump began to speak, welcoming the reporters and saying, "Thank you very much for coming and these four very courageous women have asked to be here and they are each going to make a short statement." My heart began to pound. What? We really hadn't asked to be here. We were invited to be here and had not been told about the reporters or that we would be asked to make a statement. Don't get me wrong, I had no problem making a statement. I just wish I had known about it beforehand so I could have been better prepared. We had been told nothing except that we were going to meet Mr. Trump before going to the debate. Maybe it was planned this way or maybe someone failed to tell us we would be asked to make a statement. Either way, I was glad I wasn't first. My mind was racing. What on earth was I to say? I learned earlier in the day that Mr. Trump had re-tweeted my tweet about "action speaking louder than words." I decided rather quickly that's where I needed to go with my statement.

It began with Paula, then Kathy, then me and finally Kathleen. Kathleen said later, "thank God I was last and had a little time to think." Her statement was profound and a perfect ending to all of ours. Mr. Trump then thanked the reporters for being there and the barrage of questions started. Many were shouting questions about the video and tape recorded remarks Trump had made in 2005. Trump ignored the questions as the reporters were being ushered out the door, but Paula didn't. She shouted back at them, "Why don't you ask Bill Clinton that?" Good for her.

It was over and Mr. Trumped thanked us and left the room. Kathleen and I looked at each other in bewildered amazement. What had just happened? But there was no time to discuss it. We were taken back to the basement loading area and placed in SUVs for the motorcade drive to the debate at Washington University. The interstate had been temporarily closed except for Trump's motorcade of about 8 or 10 vehicles and dozens of police cars keeping other traffic off the highway until we passed. I took a short video of the motorcade ride and all the flashing lights along the route and sent it to my grandson. He loved it. A few months earlier his father and I had told him about what happened to me in 1978. We had no choice. He had a smart phone and a MacBook and would eventually read about it.

When we arrived at the debate at Washington University we were taken to a room with "more" food and drinks. When we walked in, Mr. Trump's children and Melania were there, along with Rudy Giuliani, Steve Bannon, Kellyanne Conway and many others whose faces I had seen on television, but did not recall their names. I wish I could have paused and soaked in this moment in time, but everything was moving so quickly. The Trump family, as well as the others, were so gracious to us and expressed appreciation for our being there. Here we were in the midst of this very sophisticated and powerful family and all of the people connected to Trump's campaign and to tell you the truth, I was awe struck.

There seem to be some confusion as to where we were going to be seated. We learned the next day that Rudy Giuliani was trying to seat us with Bill Clinton, but the debate officials would not allow it. If anyone had told me I was to be seated anywhere near Bill Clinton, I would have refused. It was bad enough being in the same building with him. In a short while, Kathleen, Kathy Shelton and I were taken to our seats. Paula was late. She had gone directly from the airport to Trump's hotel in jeans and ball cap for our meeting with him. She then had to hurriedly dress for the debate. She came in just as debate was beginning.

There was a platform of cameras facing the stage. This platform was in front of the area where we were to be seated. As soon as we entered the room and started walking to our seats, all of the cameras turned on us and started filming and snapping photos as we walked to our seats. All the clicking sounded like an old electric typewriter. The cameras stayed on us until the debate introductions began. This was very uncomfortable and somewhat embarrassing. I had started taking a video with my iPhone when a security person told me I couldn't. I managed to get a few seconds, showing our proximity to where Bill Clinton was seated, the camera platform and the stage. Our seats did not face the stage. We had to pivot in our seats and look to the right through a space between the camera platform and a large American flag to see the stage.

It was surreal. Family members of the candidates, debate moderators and officials were introduced. Then came the introduction of Donald Trump and Hillary Clinton. I was nervous for Donald Trump. So much was on the line and I hoped our (Kathleen, Paula, Kathy and I) presence would make a difference. It began. Here we were, in person, watching an epic battle of words between two fierce competitors. The audience seemed equally distributed between Clinton and Trump supporters. From our vantage point, we could not see Trump and Hillary very well, but we could hear them perfectly. Before I knew it, it was over. I felt like Trump had won the debate.

When the debate was over, we were ushered back to the same room where we had started. Kellyanne Conway came over to me and ask me to go to the "spin room" with her. I had no know what a spin room was, but I obligingly went with her. It was like a boxing ring, with reporters and cameras crowding in on all sides. Reporters from every media outlet imaginable were represented. Reporters began shouting my name, "Juanita, can we talk to you?" I can see why it's called the spin room. It's so confusing with everyone talking at once to get your attention. Kellyanne stopped at the Fox News cubicle for a sit down with Megyn Kelly. I did not care for Megyn and didn't want to be in her presence so I continued around the room on my own. It was so crowded and I was wondering where Paula and Kathleen were. Then I saw Kathleen talking with reporters on the other side of the room.

Most of the questions had to do with, "How could I support Donald Trump after the disparaging remarks he made about women?" I would answer, "How could anyone support a woman who threatened and intimidated the victims of her husband?" After making my way around the room and answering questions from about a dozen or so reporters, I was about to exit the room. On the very end by the exit was a crew from NBC, saying my name and wanting me to stop and talk to them. I told them absolutely not and walked past them. There was no way I would talk to NBC, not only because of the way they had handled my Dateline interview in 1999, but also because of the recent Andrea Mitchell fiasco on the Today Show.

Kathleen and I left the spin room and returned to the refreshment room. We took photos with Rudy Giuliani, Steve Bannon, and others and continued to visit with everyone. We all were ecstatic regarding Trump's performance. The room was filled with positive emotions. Finally it was time to call it a night and go back to the hotel. What a memorable night it had been. I was exhausted from all the travel and very little sleep in the last 48 hours and welcomed the thought of going to bed. How could so much have happened in such a short period of time and how on earth did I manage to get through it? I was relieved it was over and was glad I would be heading home the next morning.

TIME TO VOTE

I tried to stay positive about Trump's possibilities of winning, but it was hard. Poll after poll would show Trump gaining but Hillary still maintaining a lead. Focus groups were leaning toward Clinton. The liberal media was hard at work against Trump and it seem to be working. But still, I felt good about going to the second debate and having my final say about the Clintons. I was still tweeting and supporting Trump in every way I knew how but in the back of my mind I was doubtful of a Trump victory. Most of my life, I had watched the Clintons wiggle out of controversy after controversy. I felt 2016 would be no different. These people were indestructible.

November 8, 2016 was finally here and I was anxious to vote. There was a line when I arrived. I had to wait for about an hour before I could vote. Everyone in line was talking about Trump and it was all positive. This was encouraging. I remembered eight years previously, I had voted for Barack Obama and I had also contributed to his campaign in the hope he would defeat Hillary in the primary and he did. I wasn't a big fan of Obama or McCain. I thought they were both weak candidates but I voted for Obama. I hate to admit it, but I didn't vote in the 2012. I was disappointed in Obama's first four years and not interested in the election process at all.

My son called and said he was having a get together at his home to watch the election returns and he would like for me to come. I told him I wasn't feeling well and would just stay home. The truth was that I needed to be alone to watch the results as they came in. It was so personal to me. The thought of Hillary Clinton winning was more than I could possibly bear and I didn't want to be around other people if and/or when it was announced. It's hard to explain. The exit poll were dribbling in and showed Clinton with a majority. The major networks, except for Fox, were positive Hillary would win. Hillary was convinced she was going to win, too.

As the night progressed, Trump began to slowly increase his lead over Clinton. All of a sudden, it was announced that Trump won Florida.....then, Wisconsin.... then Pennsylvania. The impossible was happening and my heart was pounding. Trump had penetrated the Blue Wall. I screamed and jumped as high as an overweight 73 year old woman can jump. Now I was glued to the television set. I stayed up until past 2 a.m. until I was sure he had won and Hillary had conceded. The man who ran the most unconventional campaign and defied every political rule that existed had just been elected President of the United States. Hallelujah!! Thank the good Lord, the Clintons were history and I was going to bed.

Twitter: November 9, 2016 Juanita Broaddrick @atensnut tweeted the following
Tears of Joy. Vindication after 38 years of pain and suffering. Thanks to Mr. Trump & all of you. It does go away.

When I woke, I felt like a huge weight had been lifted from my body. I hadn't felt like this in decades. It was glorious. The Clintons were no longer a part of my life. They had taken all they could from me and now they were gone. I couldn't believe it. Donald J. Trump was going to be the 45th President of the United States and my life had changed forever, for the better.

THE INAUGURATION

We were told by two different people close to the Trump organization that our invitations to the inauguration of President Donald J. Trump were going to be mailed to us (Kathleen Willey, Paula Jones McFadden and I). It was January 13, 2017 and none of us had received an invitation. I was feeling depressed and forgotten. It's difficult to explain. All three of us felt like we deserved to be a part of this monumental event. We had supported Mr. Trump and appeared at the second debate at his request. What was going on? I guess we will never know. (A side note: I did receive an invitation in the mail on March 1, 2017.)

We truly could not believe we had been overlooked. I am not trying to catapult our value as a catalyst in the election of Donald Trump.........wait, that is exactly what I am doing. Our appearance at the October 9, 2016 Presidential debate was a turning point in the campaign for Mr. Trump. The embarrassing Billy Bush recording/video was devastating to Trump's campaign. Our appearance and comments prior to the debate said to the American voters, "Okay, Trump was definitely way out of line with his comments from 2005, but the past actions of Bill and Hillary Clinton completely outweighed Donald Trump's words." Donald Trump dared to do what others would not do. He brought Bill Clinton's crimes against women and Hillary Clinton's enabling to the forefront of the campaign where they rightfully belonged.

Through the good graces of a popular TV host, Kathleen, Paula and I were invited, with expenses paid, to DC for inaugural events. I will forever be grateful to him. At first I did not want to attend in this "back door" fashion. I still felt rejected by not being formally invited by the Trump organization. He told us that he had personally spoken with Mr. Trump about this oversight and Mr. Trump had thanked him for taking care of us. This helped my wounded spirits somewhat and I decided to go.

During the campaign of 2016, we told my 13 year old grandson about my rape by Bill Clinton. He had an iPhone and iPad and would learn on his own and probably already knew. He became a huge Trump supporter. After the election, I told him, feeling sure I would be invited to the inauguration, that I would take him with me. He talked about it all the time. When the invitation never arrived, I could see his disappointment growing each day as January 20th got closer. I went to his home on January 18th to tell him I was going, but could not take him and it absolutely broke my heart. If I could have sent him in my place, I would have.

Paula Jones McFadden and I traveled to Washington, DC, together. She was fearful of flying and her husband was unable to accompany her. I drove to Little Rock, very early, on the morning of January 19th and we departed for DC. Kathleen Willey was unable to go due to a severe case of bronchitis. I was so disappointed she would not be with us.

Our first event was a Gala at the Loews Madison Hotel, for Trump contributors. It was spectacular. Paula and I wandered through the crowd to various large rooms with an unbelievable array of hors d'oeuvre and drinks. We did not know any of the people there, except for Lauren Scirocco, who is an assistant to Sean Hannity. We had become acquainted with her throughout 2016 when we appeared on Sean's radio show. Many people came up to us, introducing themselves and expressing appreciation for our support of Donald Trump. Many wanted photos with us and we happily obliged.

The event featured country artists, "Big & Rich." They were awesome and their music reverberated throughout all of the rooms. Prior to their performance, celebrities gave short speeches rejoicing in the Trump victory. These included: Dinesh D'Souza, Dr. Dorothy Woods, widow of Benghazi hero, Ty Woods, David Clarke, John Voight, Rudy Giuliani and others. I wanted to get my photo with them, but the room was so crowded I couldn't make my way to them before they exited the room. I did snap photos of them while they were speaking and put them on my Facebook page. One by one, they expressed their jubilance and renewed hope for America with the election of Donald Trump. It was great and I was happy to be a part of this celebration of optimism.

About midnight, my age was telling me it was time to return to our hotel and retire for the night. Paula is much younger and energetic and wanted to stay longer at the event, so I went to the hotel alone. I had gotten up at 4 a.m. and driven to Little Rock, which is about 2 1/2 hours from my home, boarded a plane for DC at 7a.m. and had been awake the rest of the day excitedly preparing for our attendance at this event. I think I went to sleep as soon as my head hit the pillow.

The event I wanted to attend the most was the actual inauguration of Donald Trump. This is the event that meant the most to me....the one I had promised to take my grandson to. Paula and I did not have tickets and were told we would not be able to get close enough to truly see the swearing in. I was disappointed and watched it in my hotel room on the television. I had to be satisfied with being able to attend other functions and I was looking forward to the Liberty Ball that evening.

It was difficult getting to the Liberty Ball. Our taxi driver had to let us out 6 long blocks from where the event was being held. We joined hundreds of others in their ball gowns and tuxedos making our way through police barricades keeping protestors away from us. Paula's gown was longer in the back and people kept stepping on it as we made our way down the street. I had worn comfortable shoes, but Paula had on heels and it wasn't long before she was in pain, but she trudged on. We would hear shouts of degradation from protestors throughout our long walk through the barricades to the ball. We finally arrived at the security check station and were admitted to the building. I was so relieved to be away from the protestors. They were so intimidating.

Once inside, we began to take photos of each other and, again, people would come up to us asking for photos with us. That was nice and we were happy to do so. I had done an interview on the Howie Carr radio show and his assistant had messaged me a few days before the inauguration and told me that Howie and his wife would be at the Liberty Ball. I told him I would be there, too. As soon as we got inside, he messaged me and told me where they were and to come and join them. He said they had a perfect spot at the stage where Trump would appear. Paula and I got a glass of wine and headed his way. We found him and he was right. He had a great vantage point to watch President Trump and Melania's entrance.

We visited with everyone and watched the entertainment, anticipating the arrival of the Trumps. Then, it was time for the main event. The music played and our new president and his wife walked onto the stage. It was fantastic, it was spectacular and so much more. I hadn't gotten to see the swearing in, but this was a close second. The crowd went wild. Here stood our 45th President of the United States and the First Lady. I was so proud to be a part of it. Soon, the rest of the Trump family appeared and they all danced to Frank Sinatra's "My Way." There could not have been a more appropriate song for the occasion. I wanted to cry. I wanted to shout, Hallelujah. It was a truly joyous celebration that culminated the most controversial presidential campaign and election of all time. I was finally at peace and the Clintons were history.

EPILOGUE

I wanted to write this book to tell about my life as a struggling young nurse and business woman starting in the 1960s. But, if this book does publish and sell, I know it will be because of one powerful man's assault on me. This salacious and scandalous episode in my life has become a part of history and will be discussed for years to come. I can only hope the readers will enjoy reading about my struggles and success as a young female entrepreneur because it was quite an exciting adventure.

I have been approached by writers and publishers to write a book, but they only wanted my life story that involved Bill Clinton. This is exactly what I did not want. I did not want my life to be defined merely as a victim of rape by a powerful man. I am more than that. After writing my story, the memories of the pain I suffered on April 25, 1978, are fading. I am closing the chapter on Bill and Hillary Clinton. I am happy, healthy, enjoying life.....and I have a tennis match to play.

Made in the USA
Middletown, DE
04 January 2024

47224011R00062